Overcoming Church Hurts

And Moving Forward in God

To Sharel:
Thank you for your
lovely spirit.
Cinda

by

CINDA ADAMS GASKIN

ISBN-13: 978-0692279175

ISBN-10: 0692279172

CopyLove Publishing

Printed in the United States of America

TABLE OF CONTENTS

WHY I WROTE THIS BOOK

I wrote this book to help hurting people navigate the shipwrecked waters of a church hurt. My aim is to help other believers hold on to their faith, rebuild their trust and transform the bitterness they are likely feeling into a sense of wholesomeness and peace. This book is a prescription for people hurt by the church. It is intended to offer them a new perspective on how to interact with the Body of Christ.

As someone wounded by the church, you are likely estranged from the people of God. And sadly, this is just the way the enemy would have it. As you read this book, you will discover that Satan, the enemy of your soul and the enemy of the church, wants nothing more than to isolate you while simultaneously giving the church a nice, juicy black eye. In other words, it is Satan's desire to foster division while characterizing the church within society as a place fueled by hypocrisy.

Let me caution you: this book is *not* intended to exonerate church leaders or church members from behaving in an ungodly manner; nor is it about telling you to suck it up, get back in there and continue being a good solider for the Lord. Rather, this book is about equipping you to embrace the maturity God wants to give you in exchange for your pain.

Certainly, it's difficult to imagine that on the other side of your hurt is a gift called maturity. But, as you read this book with the goal of being healed and moving forward in God, you'll discover that maturity is an attainable by-product of a church hurt. But an important condition of receiving the gift of maturity is that you have to be *willing* to receive it. And by reading this book, you are deliberately enrolling into a plan to take the necessary steps toward earning that gift.

Similar to what happens when you enroll into a school or study program, certain steps are required—known as prerequisites—before you earn the diploma or certificate of completion. In an academic setting, these steps usually encompass reading, research, homework and proving to the instructor that you have some fluency with the subject you've learned. And when you complete your studies, you willingly accept your diploma because you've *earned* it by taking the steps needed to achieve it.

I invite you to use this book as a tool—along with the Scriptures—as a manual for earning the certificate of maturity in this area of your walk with the Lord, Jesus Christ. And although the idea of overcoming your church hurt may feel like an impossible mission on this side of your pain, my prayer is that this book will strengthen your faith and that your faith will trump your feelings so that you can move on in God. I want to help you move past the pain and sidestep the aim of the enemy to isolate you and to destroy you spiritually.

You have so much to offer to the church—your gifts, your ideas, your commitment and more. But a church hurt will cause you to withhold these assets, thereby stunting the overall growth of the Body of Christ.

Right now you may be thinking, *'Yeah, but you don't know what they did to me.'* And you're right. I don't know the particular details of your story. But I can identify with the beginning, middle and end of your story as it stands right now. My goal with this book is to rewrite the ending of this season in your life. Rather than have it end on a sour note that leaves you bitter, angry and in emotional turmoil, I trust that God will speak to you through these chapters and that the Holy Spirit will lovingly compel you to let go of your story and let Him use you for His glory despite whatever "they" did.

Think about it. Isn't that what our Lord and Savior, Jesus Christ did? He was betrayed by Judas Iscariot, someone he had walked with in ministry. Peter, another member of His ministry, denied knowing

Him. And, even though He healed the sick and raised the dead, the crowd who He had sacrificially served chose Him to be crucified instead of Barabbas, who was in prison charged with murder. So, when you think about Jesus, you're in very good company in dealing with a church hurt.

We will explore the way Jesus handled these hurts and work toward applying His example in your life to help you gain the strength, freedom and deliverance needed to become more than a conqueror through Him who loves us.

WHY YOU SHOULD
READ THIS BOOK

You should read this book because you're hurting or you know someone else who is. And, as the saying goes, hurt people hurt people. Rather than going through life with unresolved pain that can negatively affect others, allow this book to help you gain a proactive stance toward your healing.

Taking a proactive approach means you leverage every opportunity to release the hurt so that you can reach a better place in God.

Another reason you should read this book is to protect yourself and others from experiencing the type of hurt you're feeling right now. How better to do that than to understand how you arrived at this place of pain to begin with.

Think about a time when you were lost during a car trip. Once you discovered the wrong turns you took and learned the right route for reaching your destination, you willingly shared that with others coming behind you, right? Of course you did. We all do that. The key is sharing the dos and don'ts in a constructive and edifying way—not in a way that brings dishonor to the Body of Christ. Reading this book will help you set a godly barometer in how you lead others in walking through the minefield of potential church hurts.

Reading this book will also help you regain your power—that sense of personal and spiritual confidence and leadership that compels you to participate fully in the kingdom of God. When you're sidelined by a church hurt, it's likely that you feel stripped of the enthusiasm you once exhibited toward the ministry. Even your zeal toward the Lord can become dry and lifeless. This book is intended to refresh you—

like rain after a drought—so that you can begin to grow, blossom and bear fruit once again.

Finally, you should read this book so that you can lead others to Christ from a place of strength borne out of love, empathy for the frailty of the human condition and forgiveness. Again, this is merely following the example of Jesus Christ. After Jesus was betrayed by Judas Iscariot and one of his disciples cut off the ear of the priest's guard, Jesus said:

> *"Do you think I cannot call on my Father, and he will at once put at my disposal more than twelve legions of angels? But how then would the Scriptures be fulfilled that say it must happen in this way?"*

> - Matthew 26:53-54 (NIV)

Here, we read that Jesus could have used His power in an undisciplined way to annihilate His accusers along with the one who had betrayed Him. Yet, He didn't because He knew that there was something much bigger at stake than revenge, and that was the salvation of the world. Jesus chose to focus His attention on the will of God rather than soothing His hurt at that moment.

Similarly, you have a choice to make about how you will respond to your church hurt. You, too, have a bigger responsibility than revenge. As a believer in Jesus Christ, you have been commissioned by Him to invite others to partake of the glorious salvation that cleanses us from sin and offers us eternal life. By reading this book, you are giving greater weight to your responsibility to The Great Commission than to your hurt.

This book is not intended to ignore or subjugate your pain. Rather, it is intended to stigmatize the perpetuation of pain within the church so that fewer people become casualties who leave the church and subsequently fall away from the faith.

Reading this book will not only support you in boldly standing for righteousness in a new and enlightened way, but will offer you a firm footing of faith in God—rather than in people—that will strengthen those you lead into the kingdom to quickly overcome the church hurts they may one day face.

CHAPTER 1

WHAT IS A CHURCH HURT?

I have often heard believers somberly say, "There's no hurt like a church hurt!" I didn't really understand what that meant until I found myself dealing with a church hurt of my own. I had gone from someone who was the enthusiastic go-to person at my church to someone who felt chained to a building and a leadership that was suddenly foreign to me.

After serving in a ministry for 19 years, and spending 12 of those years as a church staff member, I was left nursing a church hurt that rendered me bitter, angry, distrustful of church leadership and emotionally traumatized.

I traveled 50 miles each way to work five days a week for the last five years of my employment at my former church. And during the last few years of those stressful days, I'd cry all the way to work and all the way home. I'd often mix in prayer, too, but my heart was broken, my faith was damaged and it was difficult for me to trust God. *'Why wasn't He protecting me?'* I wondered. *'And why was He allowing me to go through this?'*

During those final years of my church staff employment, I vigorously searched for other jobs, but the economic downturn in the U.S. was raging, and landing a position required nothing short of divine intervention. Plus, my résumé showed more than ten years of ministry work, which would have been great if I wanted to move on to another ministry, but I didn't. I desperately wanted to work in a place that had nothing to do with my spiritual life. My heart was screaming for a separation of church and state in that the messiness of my church hurt was bleeding into other areas of my life, and I wanted to ensure that that never happened to me again.

My children were the first to notice the change in me. They tried to console me whenever I broke down at home because of the latest antics of my nemesis at work. He had the position, power and authority to ruin me, and he was ruthlessly pursuing every avenue to achieve his goal. And it both shocked and saddened me that the senior leader turned a blind eye to these shenanigans. He seemed oblivious to the pain this one person was causing—not only me, but others on staff.

Because of the reverential nature of working for a pastoral team within a church and ministry, it is often difficult to speak up boldly when injustices occur. Often, within church culture, common folk— the regular church members—are viewed as lower on the totem pole of value than those in leadership. This perception typically leaves complaints by regular members unaddressed. But church hurts are not limited to the people in the pews.

Leaders also suffer from hurts dished out by other leaders or church members. I recall a time when my former pastor was saddened by long-term leaders leaving the church without so much as a good-bye. He seemed genuinely crushed by the folks who had left under those terms. And, I'm aware that there are a myriad of stories involving pastors who have been hurt by church members, but sadly, in the case of church hurts, typically the person with most power wins.

As we explore church hurts, I want to provide you with a definition of a church hurt. I also want to help you to understand what just happened to you. Often, when we're blindsided by an unfortunate and painful outcome, we are so inundated with the emotions of the situation that it's difficult to clearly see what actually happened. My goal is to help you gain the clarity you need to help you move forward with God. The last thing I want you to do is to allow this mishap to waylay your faith and spiritual growth.

As we walk through this chapter together, I invite you to follow the words of Paul in Hebrews 12:1-4 where the apostle admonishes us to lay aside every weight and the sin that so easily besets us. Let's read these verses from the New King James Version:

> Therefore we also, since we are surrounded by so great a cloud of witnesses, let us lay aside every weight, and the sin which so easily ensnares *us*, and let us run with endurance the race that is set before us, [2] looking unto Jesus, the author and finisher of *our* faith, who for the joy that was set before Him endured the cross, despising the shame, and has sat down at the right hand of the throne of God.

> [3] For consider Him who endured such hostility from sinners against Himself, lest you become weary and discouraged in your souls. 4 You have not yet resisted to bloodshed, striving against sin.

Based on these verses and my goal to see you strengthened, I want you to take that heavy boulder of pain you've been carrying around and lay it aside as you read this chapter. This may seem like an impossible feat to you at the moment, but just give it a shot.

Imagine that you are planning a wonderful picnic with someone you are romantically involved with. You have prepared everything—the food and drinks, the music, the tableware and recreation. Then, just as you and your loved one set out for the park, the sky darkens and a huge thunderstorm hits. You have to call off the picnic. Sure, you're disappointed, but there's nothing you can do about it. No one can control the weather. And even if you wait until the storm ends, the ground will be wet. You have no other choice but to postpone it for another day.

But you and your sweetheart don't have to call off the entire day. The picnic is ruined, but the two of you can adjust your plans and make the best of simply being together. You can move the picnic indoors, go to a museum or take in a movie. That's how I'm asking you to approach overcoming your church hurt. I want you to see it as disappointing, but not devastating. And although it may have deeply wounded you on several levels, I want you to let go of that pain—counting it as simply something that caused you to change your plans—to remove any rationalization that can block God's healing for your life.

Once, after I was blatantly ignored by a church leader who I had worked for and who had refused to pay me, I had to simply let it go. Does that mean that I was letting go of the debt? Not at all. But I had to let go of the offense. It was weighing on me terribly. I was so attached to "getting paid," that a good part of my day was focused on that objective. I had a long laundry list of bills that needed to be paid with that money. And each day that this leader ignored my calls, I'd mentally go down that list and think about my debt, my daughter's college tuition and all the things I had expected to do with that money. And even though I had done the work and was owed the money, the bottom line is that I was miserable. I'd go to bed with it on my mind and wake up with it on my mind. But was it worth it? I decided that it wasn't, and I simply let it go. That's what I'm asking of you.

As you read this chapter and the subsequent ones, let go and let God. Now I realize that this is a time-worn expression that has lost its impact through overuse, but in this case, if you let go of the story about what happened and let God work on you and in your favor, things may just turn out for the better. Now let's define a church hurt.

What is a Church Hurt?

With all the pain going on in the world, one would think that being mishandled by a church would be low on the list of life's major challenges. Sadly, though, the wounds of a church hurt run very deep. This is because the pain of being mistreated in ministry is so multi-dimensional that it cuts across years—perhaps decades—of your life in serving a church, in building relationships with others, in

14

spiritual growth and in sharing special events with the people you've come to know as your church family.

Further, the church in society is a place that represents goodness, truth, stability and love. It's supposed to be a safe place—a place where you can interact without all the usual filters and boundaries you erect in other settings because what unites church members is God. And because God is holy, loves unconditionally, is faithful and deals with His people based upon purity of heart and righteousness, we sometimes believe that the people of God will follow suit. Not so. In fact, believing that because God is love means that the church will always love you is a major misstep in church life.

My former church used to offer a portion of the worship service that involved a brief teaching about principles related to the church. These homilies were given after the praise and worship portion of our service while the children were being dismissed to their Sunday school classes.

During these teachings, one of the leaders explained to the congregation how church members are to interact with one another and with leadership. They'd help us understand issues around giving, getting to church on time and if the pastor didn't happen to get around to saying hello to you on a Sunday morning, we shouldn't see that as a snub, but to recognize that he or she may be dealing with issues surrounding the service or other ministry-related problems. These were good "meat and potato" lessons, but none ever covered what to do when faced with a church hurt.

Defining a Church Hurt

So, let's define a church hurt. Since the dictionary doesn't provide a definition, here's the one I created and will use throughout this book: A church hurt is the emotional pain experienced by an individual or group based upon the real or perceived behaviors and actions of other church members or leaders.

Emotional pain can be devastating in any relationship. And if you've experienced a church hurt, guess what? You are in a relationship with a church. Although the church is made up of people, the church as an institution—the building, its significance, the vision and mission—becomes the symbol of pain whenever its leaders or members hurt someone or whenever there is a *perception* that the leaders or members have inflicted emotional pain on someone.

The reason I highlight the word perception is because, let's face it, not all church hurts are real. I recall once a woman wanted to sue a local church because her dress was snagged on a pew—snagged, not ripped, mind you. And even though she indicated that the dress was valued at less than $50.00, she was purportedly so "wounded" by the trauma caused by the snag on her dress that she was seeking an ungodly amount of money in retribution for her emotional suffering.

Obviously, this woman's perception of damages was skewed to say the least. My gut told me that she was merely an opportunist and had probably run the same scam elsewhere. Nonetheless, when she went to her lawyer's office to complain about the snag in her dress, I'm sure she conveyed to him or her that she was wounded by the church's negligence. Her attorney's perception of the church was affected by the woman's story and the lawyer took legal action based upon that perception.

Similarly, you may have shared your church hurt with others and their perception of the church has been affected by your story. I encourage you to be careful about sharing the story of your church hurt with the people in your life. If you are willing to go to them with a personal problem, like a church hurt, it is because these are the people in your life who care most about you. These are the people who are willing to fight for you and will likely stand with you whether you're in the right or in the wrong.

The problem is that when you share what happened between you and the church with your loved ones, it is likely that they will form very strong, negative opinions about the people who hurt you and the church itself. Your need for comfort could be the very thing that causes the person you share your pain with to stay away from the church, from God's people or from salvation itself.

Consider that being in a relationship with a church is similar to being in relationship with a person. If you tell everyone in your family or close circle of friends about the various mishaps between you and your significant other, you may distance those people from your partner and never regain their trust of him or her.

While the concept of being in a relationship with a church may be radical to some, joining a church and becoming "involved" happens in degrees, just the way interpersonal relationships develop.

I had been a member of one church for 19 years. And the pastor often invited people to join the church by jokingly saying, "You've been dating the church long enough. Now it's time to make a commitment!" And as I heard these words, knowing that I had eagerly made such a commitment years earlier, what I understood from this running joke was that my relationship with the church was not only important to my pastor, but important to God. The underlying communication was that people were toying with God and not taking Him seriously by neglecting to join the church. But, later, after people joined or became frequent visitors, they often began introducing their friends and families to the church. In your case, you may have even invited co-workers or neighbors to attend church with you at some point.

For most active church members, a significant amount of time is spent at church. Often, attending midweek services, church meetings and Sunday services could mean being at church at least two to three times a week. And when you're at church that regularly, you and members of your household become fixtures of the church. People expect to see you there. You become knowledgeable about the inner workings of the church, from the physical building to the church's plans and policies. And like in a relationship you have with a person, when you spend two to three times a week with that person, introduce your family and associates to that person and get to know them on various levels—it's a relationship.

Similar to any other relationship, you expect to be cared for, loved and protected in church. And because the church is a place where people protect each other from the ills of life away from God, many of us drop our guards and go about our service to the church wearing the proverbial rose-colored glasses. That means we don't put the proper boundaries in place to ensure that we don't get hurt. Let's explore what happens when a church hurt occurs.

What Just Happened?

As the saying goes, there are no new stories in the world. What that means is that all stories are pretty much the same with different reiterations on the basic structure of a story. This is also true when it comes to the back story of your church hurt.

While it may be excruciatingly painful to you, believe it or not, your story is a lot like millions of others. This in no way is intended to diminish what you've been through. Rather, it is intended to defuse the magnitude of your pain and help you to see that you're not alone. The details and complexity of your story are unique, but the set up—how the church hurt began in the first place—the conflict and its resolution are pretty much all the same.

Let's compare what typically happens in a church hurt to a story that we're all familiar with. In Little Red Riding Hood, by The Brothers Grim, the main character is doing a good deed in taking her sick Grandma a basket full of food. Along the way, she encounters the Big Bad Wolf who wants to eat Little Red. He runs ahead of her, eats Grandma and lays in wait to also eat the unsuspecting girl. In the classic tale, the wolf devours Little Red and a passing huntsman hears the overstuffed wolf snoring at Grandma's house. He comes in and cuts his stomach open, freeing Little Red and Grandma.

In your story, what likely happened is you were doing a number of good deeds by serving at your church. You encounter someone with bad motives—someone who devises a plan to take you down. Perhaps that wasn't their original idea, but that was the direction of their heart. The first thing the person with bad motives does is go after your ministry—the thing you were doing before the conflict began. Even if you weren't holding any official title in ministry, the person with wrong motives wanted to destroy your future by somehow attacking your family or reputation. You were, in fact, emotionally and perhaps spiritually devastated by the outcome of these events. That's where we are at this point in your story. Jesus, the Redeemer, characterized as the Huntsman here, is on the way to freeing you.

Sadly, most church hurts follow this pattern. In my own church hurt, there was one person who didn't seem to like my independence in ministry. He wanted to control the area of ministry I had been given purview over. He even assigned his close relative—who had no formal training or experience in my area—to work with me to ensure he'd get the "inside scoop." He also began a smear campaign to turn other co-workers against me. Some took the bait. I eventually left the ministry and all those he temporarily beguiled left, too.

Another friend of mine suffered a church hurt whereby she was serving in ministry for years in a very public position. She spoke her mind to a ministry leader who had the power to unilaterally remove her from ministry and suddenly she was gone. Because of the public nature of her ministry, an explanation was needed for her sudden departure. The church bid her farewell with a special service that she tearfully endured all the while feeling that she was railroaded out of her position. Further, she was mortified before people who had previously looked up to her as a ministry leader.

Another friend ended up on the wrong side of a ministry leader—one who had initially been setting her up to take down another unsuspecting ministry leader. He had been sending her to meetings that she hadn't previously been part of to be the "mole" on his behalf and to see that his objectives were carried out. The person who was originally holding the position became weary that my friend was suddenly encroaching upon her turf and made some noise about it to the senior leader. The plan was delayed a bit, but during that downtime, my friend and the ringleader butted heads and my friend was unceremoniously fired from ministry.

In another story, one ministry leader, who had been the darling of the ministry because he was responsible for reviving a dying area of ministry was seemingly marginalized by the senior pastor based on envy. Because the area of ministry he revitalized became so immediately popular, the senior pastor began regularly suspending him from oversight of that ministry using trumped up charges to rationalize his behavior. After a series of suspensions—some without pay—the ministry leader left the ministry brokenhearted.

In yet another case, one ministry leader shared with another his plans to leave the church where they both worked. The first leader was frustrated about various aspects of how the church operated. When the senior pastor got wind of the plan, he called in the person who was given the information and asked, "Why didn't you tell me he wanted to leave?" The ministry leader explained that he didn't feel comfortable sharing his friend's sentiments because it may have just been "talk." The angry senior pastor told him that if the frustrated leader did leave the ministry, he would pray relentlessly that God punish the man who withheld this pertinent information from him. That leader left the ministry.

Finally, a ministry leader and his wife were divorcing. Because the wife ended the marriage with more financial clout, the ministry's leaders said they were "neutral" when the former husband asked them to intervene and speak to her about allowing him to visit with the children. The leaders told him that they couldn't get involved. The former husband, who had counseled other couples at the church as an elder, had himself been instructed to support other couples regarding such issues in the past. He surmised that rather than losing his ex-wife's financial support, the church chose to neglect his request. He subsequently left the ministry and was ordained within a different denomination.

In reading these stories, the emotional pain suffered by the person involved may be lost in the translation. Similarly, when you relay your story to others, the impact of your pain may be lost as well. This is because *you* own your pain. Certainly people can empathize with you, but only you feel the full thrust of the details of what's happened to you. Only you know how close you were to the members you are now leaving. Only you know how you babysat for their children or spent weeks going to visit them in the hospital, only to have them become "neutral" or turn their backs on you altogether so as not to lose their own footing in ministry.

So what's the big deal? Why so much drama surrounding church hurts that read as benign to onlookers? For the Believer, church attendance is as foundational as a residence is to a marriage. Church is where we learn how to "do" Christianity. It's the place where we are taught—presumably from someone who is spiritually mature and someone gifted to not only teach Scripture, but to exemplify godliness—how to live out our faith. At church we also learn the characteristics of God, how to pray, how to interact with church leaders and peers, how to worship and pray in a corporate setting, how to serve others and how to give. We also are given tremendous opportunities to learn new skills and develop our spiritual and natural gifts—ranging from camera work, administrative tasks and interior decorating to singing in the choir, performing in a step team and bookkeeping.

Further, we bring the skills we developed professionally to the fore at church. I used my skills as a writer to eventually become associate director of marketing and communications at my church, a job that included producing a myriad of promotional and informational videos, a weekly television broadcast, daily radio show, edited some

14 books, several manuals, wrote copy for over 10 annual reports and several reiterations of web content.

The church is a wonderful place for relational growth and development as well. Aside from experiencing deep and meaningful friendships with people of like precious faith, marriages are often cultivated out of the connection of shared faith and values between people who join together at a particular place of worship. And the church is often a place where the needs of an entire family can be met. Often, churches serve every member of the family—from infants and children to teens and young adults all the way up to married people and senior adults.

But when a church hurt occurs, having all this deeply identifying affiliation ripped away on the ugly contrivance of personal conflict is a painful and confusing experience. It affects you on several levels. First, it affects your relationships at church. When you're hurt, you want those close to you to feel your pain—at least to acknowledge the wrong that's been done to you. We have previously discussed the pitfalls of sharing your church hurt with the people who love you most—not always a good idea.

Further, if you're a staff member or a paid weekly worker, as some part-time church musicians are, a church hurt can affect you financially. It's almost always challenging to lose even a portion of your livelihood. But when losing your job is mixed with losing a respected role in the church, losing relationships that are important to you and losing faith in the leadership at your church, it is very likely that the person experiencing the hurt will also be challenged to continue walking with God.

As we continue unpacking the trauma of a church hurt, our next step will be to discover why church hurts occur.

CHAPTER 2

WHY CHURCH HURTS HAPPEN

In January 2013, christianitytoday.com[1] posted an article titled "Deaths from church attacks rise 36 percent in 2012." Citing data from church security expert Carl Chinn, the article reported 75 deaths from attacks at faith-based organizations in 2012. It further adds Chinn's statistic of 135 deadly force incidents that occurred in churches and faith-based organizations in 2012.

In late September 2013, a deacon from a Lake Charles, Louisiana church walked into his church and allegedly shot the pastor, killing him as he stood before some 60 members of his congregation during a Friday night revival service. As the story unfolded in the days that ensued, it was reported that the deacon's wife had filed rape charges against the pastor two days before the shooting.

The rising statistics surrounding deadly, violent incidents occurring at churches indicate that church hurts are very serious issues that sometimes destroy families and end lives. But what's the reason for these murderous outbursts in churches? What causes people who clearly desire to know God and who seemingly desire to live godly lives to commit such egregious acts of violence?

My 19 years within one ministry and a spattering of years in a few others have taught me that despite the quality of ministry, the training of the pastor or the socio-economic status of the congregants, church hurts occur for three main reasons: the flesh, the world and

---

[1] http://www.christianitytoday.com/gleanings/2013/january/deaths-from-church-attacks-rise-36-in-2012.html

the devil. In this chapter we will explore the role these three elements play in church hurts.

While I recognize that these three reasons may appear to be a bit cliché, as we delve into them, I trust you will find that each one—or some combination of them—is at the center of your church hurt.

Even though you can point to the person who hurt you, let me remind you of what the Apostle Paul said in Ephesians 6:12.

> Finally, my brethren, be strong in the Lord and in the power of His might. 11 Put on the whole armor of God, that you may be able to stand against the wiles of the devil. 12 For we do not wrestle against flesh and blood, but against principalities, against powers, against the rulers of the darkness of this age,[c] against spiritual hosts of wickedness in the heavenly places.

Here, the great apostle helps us to see that it's not *people* who are causing us trouble, but principalities, powers and the rulers of the darkness of this age. And while I understand that "she" really did do this or "he" really did do that, I also know that the goal of the enemy is to sow seeds of division between you and other believers. For the remainder of this chapter, let's look at the first of these three areas where church hurts are rooted.

The Flesh

How does one define the flesh? It represents the carnal nature of man. The flesh embodies those passions, appetites, affinities and desires that are opposed to the character of God as represented in sacred Scripture. The by-products of the flesh are outlined in Galatians 5:17-21:

> For the desires of the flesh are against the Spirit, and the desires of the Spirit are against the flesh, for these are

opposed to each other, to keep you from doing the things you want to do. 18 But if you are led by the Spirit, you are not under the law. 19 Now the works of the flesh are evident: sexual immorality, impurity, sensuality, 20 idolatry, sorcery, enmity, strife, jealousy, fits of anger, rivalries, dissensions, divisions, 21 envy,[d] drunkenness, orgies, and things like these. I warn you, as I warned you before, that those who do such things will not inherit the kingdom of God.

These verses list sexual immorality, impurity, sensuality, idolatry, sorcery, enmity, strife, jealousy, fits of anger, rivalries, dissensions, divisions, envy, drunkenness, orgies and such as resulting from fleshly behaviors. And one or more of these behaviors is typically at play when a church hurt occurs. But how do people who are filled with the Holy Spirit, presumably spending time in prayer and publicly receiving a steady diet of Bible teaching, end up fulfilling these works of the flesh?

My theory is that our sin nature—the flesh—is inextricably foundational to the human experience and becomes triggered based upon an egotistical response to certain stimuli. These stimuli elicit the works of the flesh, namely enmity, jealousy, fits of anger, sexual immorality and the like. And while these responses can be overcome, even in the face of emotionally volatile stimuli, our sin nature is so instinctive that the eventual reaction is typically relegated to the flesh. I believe these reactions are initially masked by the acquired "right-thing-to-do" Christian response, however.

On *The Steve Harvey Morning Show* radio show, his nephew, Thomas Miles, a.k.a. "Nephew Tommy," has a segment called "The Prank Call." He calls someone with what at first appears to be a serious issue—for instance, indicating that their spouse has left a hotel key in a coat pocket at the dry cleaners—gets them all riled up and eventually lets them know that a friend or family member set them up to receive a prank call. Tommy often calls Christians who quickly put Jesus aside to deal with the issue at hand on their own.

One day, I listened as Nephew Tommy called a man who was about to have surgery. Tommy was claiming to be a new deacon at the man's church calling to offer prayer for the success of the upcoming surgery. During the prayer, Tommy—as the fake deacon—began saying a very nice prayer, adding that God protect the man's kidneys. The man interrupted him, saying that his kidneys were fine and that he didn't need prayer for his kidneys. With that, Tommy informed him that *he* actually needed a kidney and was hoping that while the surgeon had the man open, he'd consent to donating one of his kidneys to Tommy.

Well, it didn't take the man very long to go off. He quickly went to cursing and yelling. He was ready to fight Tommy—even though he was only days from having surgery.

The idea that Tommy had the audacity to ask someone for their kidney under the guise of prayer is simply outrageous and hysterical at the same time. But the man's reaction is typical of the Christians Tommy pulls his pranks on. In most "Prank Call" cases, the person being pranked starts out sweetly using "Praise the Lord" and "Amen" in all the right places. But as soon as Tommy hits that fleshy nerve, even the best of Christians "go there."

Once Tommy even called a pastor and told him that the pews at his church would be repossessed due to a bill he inherited from a previous pastor that went unpaid. Thankfully, the pastor who was pranked didn't use foul language, but he came pretty close—telling Tommy in no uncertain terms that he and some of the deacons would "lay hands" on anyone who came to the church to remove those pews.

Still, not everyone who experiences a church hurt goes into sin nature mode. Some believers beautifully withstand the attacks they suffer and manage to hold on to their consecration throughout the conflict. Sadly, this is not true for everyone. But what I'd like to focus upon here is the initiation of a church hurt and how the sin nature— the flesh—plays a factor in igniting these emotional firestorms.

At the outset of a church hurt, there's usually some focus on how you—the self—are being perceived or feeling. And as humans, it's very difficult to separate out the self from our redeemed Spirit-man. It seems that we are stuck in a Catch-22 in that we want to live holy, even under the most challenging circumstances, but we can't always do so.

Even the Apostle Paul acknowledged this in the book of Romans, chapter 7. Let's read verses 14-25 in *The Message* version of the Bible:

> 14-16 I can anticipate the response that is coming: "I know that all God's commands are spiritual, but I'm not. Isn't this also your experience?" Yes. I'm full of myself—after all, I've spent a long time in sin's prison. What I don't understand about myself is that I decide one way, but then I act another, doing things I absolutely despise. So if I can't be trusted to figure out what is best for myself and then do it, it becomes obvious that God's command is necessary.

> 17-20 But I need something more! For if I know the law but still can't keep it, and if the power of sin within me keeps sabotaging my best intentions, I obviously need help! I realize that I don't have what it takes. I can will it, but I can't do it. I decide to do good, but I don't really do it; I decide not to do bad, but then I do it anyway. My decisions, such as they are, don't result in actions. Something has gone wrong deep within me and gets the better of me every time.

> 21-23 It happens so regularly that it's predictable. The moment I decide to do good, sin is there to trip me up. I truly delight in God's commands, but it's pretty obvious that not all of me joins in that delight. Parts of me covertly rebel, and just when I least expect it, they take charge.

> 24 I've tried everything and nothing helps. I'm at the end of my rope. Is there no one who can do anything for me? Isn't that the real question?

25 The answer, thank God, is that Jesus Christ can and does. He acted to set things right in this life of contradictions where I want to serve God with all my heart and mind, but am pulled by the influence of sin to do something totally different.

Here, even Paul acknowledges that the sin nature often gets the best of him. And as we focus upon the initiation of the church hurt, we can see here that the sin nature is at work right from the very start of every human conflict.

I love the saying that goes, "There is no 'I' in team." But there is an "I" in individual. And when a church hurt arises, it's our individual goal of saving face, self-preservation, maintaining respect and winning the argument that's fueling our sin nature to fight. The idea that we are not warring against flesh and blood, but principalities and powers, goes out the window. The person or persons standing in opposition to our goals, or those we believe responsible for igniting our church hurt, are the target; and our anger, self-righteousness and indignation are the ammunition.

What if we recognized these facts right at the outset of a church hurt? What if we could freeze-frame the action and refer to a *Church Hurt Checklist* to determine what's happening before we get off into the flesh? What would such a list look like? Perhaps a Church Hurt Checklist would include the following:

Church Hurt Checklist

1. Did the other person's actions or statements, or the actions or statements of others, arouse a negative emotion within me?	✓
2. Do I feel the temptation arising to rebuke, put this person in his or her place or strike out in some other way?	✓

3. Will the Holy Spirit be grieved, and will the enemy rejoice at the outcome of this verbal exchange and/or my actions?	✓
4. Does this verbal exchange or response have the potential to cause a wedge in my relationship with the person, with God or with the church?	✓
5. If I don't react, will others view me as weak and a pushover? Will I view myself this way?	✓
6. If I do react, will others see me as strong and in command of the situation? Will I view myself this way?	✓
7. I feel the need to protect myself or my self-image from the other person or other people involved.	✓
8. The person I'm in conflict with should be afraid of me and should protect him- or herself from me.	✓
9. Am I willing to burn at least one relational bridge over this? Have I taken account of the potential bridges that could be burned by my actions?	✓
10. The idea of walking away from this potential fight and postponing the discussion or my actions until another time doesn't enter my mind.	✓

If you can check off one or more of the reactions listed, this is an indication that the flesh is at play and you're at risk of embarking upon a church hurt. Further, the person you're facing off against is probably experiencing the same reactions. Likely, no positive outcome will result from such flesh-to-flesh jabbing. And then there are times when only one person in the exchange is in the flesh and the other person is largely oblivious to what's brewing.

In the case of Cain and Able, it was Cain who yielded to his fleshly response of jealousy. Let's look at the checklist to assess which reactions he was likely dealing with before murdering his brother. Let's read the account in Genesis 4:1-15.

Now Adam knew Eve his wife, and she conceived and bore Cain, and said, "I have acquired a man from the Lord." 2 Then she bore again, this time his brother Abel. Now Abel was a keeper of sheep, but Cain was a tiller of the ground. 3 And in the process of time it came to pass that Cain brought an offering of the fruit of the ground to the Lord. 4 Abel also brought of the firstborn of his flock and of their fat. And the Lord respected Abel and his offering, 5 but He did not respect Cain and his offering. And Cain was very angry, and his countenance fell.

6 So the Lord said to Cain, "Why are you angry? And why has your countenance fallen? 7 If you do well, will you not be accepted? And if you do not do well, sin lies at the door. And its desire is for you, but you should rule over it."

8 Now Cain talked with Abel his brother;[a] and it came to pass, when they were in the field, that Cain rose up against Abel his brother and killed him.

9 Then the Lord said to Cain, "Where is Abel your brother?"

He said, "I do not know. Am I my brother's keeper?"

10 And He said, "What have you done? The voice of your brother's blood cries out to Me from the ground. 11 So now you are cursed from the earth, which has opened its mouth to receive your brother's blood from your hand. 12 When you till the ground, it shall no longer yield its strength to you. A fugitive and a vagabond you shall be on the earth."

13 And Cain said to the Lord, "My punishment is greater than I can bear! 14 Surely You have driven me out this day

from the face of the ground; I shall be hidden from Your face; I shall be a fugitive and a vagabond on the earth, and it will happen that anyone who finds me will kill me."

15 And the Lord said to him, "Therefore,[b] whoever kills Cain, vengeance shall be taken on him sevenfold." And the Lord set a mark on Cain, lest anyone finding him should kill him.

Cain's Church Hurt Check List

1. Did the other person's actions or statements or the actions or statements of others arouse a negative emotion within Cain? – *Yes, Cain's jealously was aroused by God's respect of Abel's offering.*	✓
2. Did Cain feel the temptation arising to rebuke, put Abel in his place or strike out in some other way? – *Yes, the Lord asked Cain, "Why are you angry? And why has your countenance fallen?" It is obvious that Cain was upset.*	✓
3. Will the Holy Spirit be grieved and will the enemy rejoice at the outcome of this verbal exchange and/or my actions? – *Yes, God warned Cain that sin was lying at the door, desiring to have dominion over Cain.*	✓
4. Did this verbal exchange or response cause a wedge in Cain's relationship with Abel or God or others? – *Yes, Cain went out to the field to talk to his brother and then rose up and killed him. His dead brother's blood cried out from the ground and God put a curse on Cain, who was worried about being hidden from God's face and that everyone who saw him would want to kill him.*	✓
5. If Cain didn't react, would others have viewed him as weak and a pushover? Would he have viewed himself this way? – *No, there is no indication that Cain struggled with how others would view him if he did not react to the situation.*	✓

6. By reacting, do others see Cain as strong and in command of the situation? Does he view himself this way? – *No, there is no indication that Cain struggled with how others would view him if he did not react to the situation. And God did not view his reaction as strong or in command; Cain lost control.*	✔
7. Does Cain feel the need to protect himself or his self-image from the other person or other people involved. – *Yes, Cain immediately lied when God asked him where his brother was. He became defensive as asked if he was his brother's keeper.*	✔
8. Should Abel have protected himself from Cain? – *Absolutely. Had Abel protected himself, he may not have been killed.*	✔
9. Was Cain willing to burn at least one relational bridge over this? – *Yes, Cain was willing to kill his brother over this situation.*	✔
10. The idea of walking away from this potential fight and postponing the discussion or his actions until another time didn't enter Cain's mind. – *No, the idea of walking away didn't enter Cain's mind.*	✔

By running down the checklist, it appears that Cain was dealing with at least 8 out of the 10 reactions provided. Notice how jealousy, anger, rage and murder were all part of Cain's reaction even before he slew his brother, Abel.

Now, let's look at David's plan to get rid of Bathsheba's husband, Uriah. You may know the story, but I'll summarize it here. David was supposed to be out fighting a war, but he stayed home in Jerusalem instead. He happened to see a beautiful woman bathing as he was out on his roof one evening. He learned that this woman was the wife of one of his warriors, Uriah, but David still sent his messengers to get the woman; he laid with her, and she conceived a child.

In an attempt to cover up the matter and have Uriah believe it was his child, David called him off the battlefield and told him to go home for a rest. David even loaded the unsuspecting Uriah down with food to take home. But because Uriah was so faithful, he refused to enjoy the pleasures of food, drink and lying with his wife while his colleagues were at war. David even went so far as to get Uriah drunk the next day to get him "in the mood" to be with his wife, but Uriah still didn't go home. Let's read the rest of the story from 2 Samuel 11:14-27.

14 In the morning it happened that David wrote a letter to Joab and sent it by the hand of Uriah. 15 And he wrote in the letter, saying, "Set Uriah in the forefront of the hottest battle, and retreat from him, that he may be struck down and die." 16 So it was, while Joab besieged the city, that he assigned Uriah to a place where he knew there were valiant men. 17 Then the men of the city came out and fought with Joab. And some of the people of the servants of David fell; and Uriah the Hittite died also.

18 Then Joab sent and told David all the things concerning the war, 19 and charged the messenger, saying, "When you have finished telling the matters of the war to the king, 20 if it happens that the king's wrath rises, and he says to you: 'Why did you approach so near to the city when you fought? Did you not know that they would shoot from the wall? 21 Who struck Abimelech the son of Jerubbesheth? [a] Was it not a woman who cast a piece of a millstone on him from the wall, so that he died in Thebez? Why did you go near the wall?'—then you shall say, 'Your servant Uriah the Hittite is dead also.'"

22 So the messenger went, and came and told David all that Joab had sent by him. 23 And the messenger said to David, "Surely the men prevailed against us and came out to us in the field; then we drove them back as far as the entrance of the gate. 24 The archers shot from the wall at your servants; and some of the king's servants are dead, and your servant Uriah the Hittite is dead also."

25 Then David said to the messenger, "Thus you shall say to Joab: 'Do not let this thing displease you, for the sword devours one as well as another. Strengthen your attack against the city, and overthrow it.' So encourage him."

26 When the wife of Uriah heard that Uriah her husband was dead, she mourned for her husband. 27 And when her mourning was over, David sent and brought her to his house, and she became his wife and bore him a son. But the thing that David had done displeased the Lord.

David was so focused on salvaging his own reputation, that he was completely blind to the utter sinfulness of his actions. He went from taking another man's wife—a man who was serving him on the battlefield—to attempting to dupe Uriah into thinking he had impregnated his wife, when David was actually the father, to eventually having the army drop back so that the enemy could kill him.

Let's look at the checklist to see if David meets the criteria for being in the flesh at the initiation of this church hurt—in that he could have turned it around before things got so out of hand.

David's "Church" Hurt Check List

1. Did Uriah's actions arouse a negative emotion within David? – *Yes, he was frustrated that Uriah didn't lie with his wife when David called him off the battlefield.*	✓
2. Did David feel the temptation arising to strike out against Uriah in some other way? – *Yes, he kept looking for a way to deceive Uriah.*	✓
3. Was the Holy Spirit grieved and did the enemy rejoice at the outcome of David's actions? – *Yes, David was God's anointed king of Israel. This certainly gave a black eye to God's people.*	✓

4. Did David's response cause a wedge in his relationship with the person, with God or others? – *Yes, David's behavior was in direct opposition to the character of God and he killed a man who had been a faithful servant of Israel.*	✓
5. If David didn't react, would others have viewed him as weak and a pushover? Would he view himself that way? – *No, David wasn't posturing for anyone else.*	✓
6. If he did react, would others see David as strong and in command of the situation? Would he view himself that way? – *No, David wanted to keep what he was doing a secret.*	✓
7. Did David feel the need to protect himself or his self-image? – *Absolutely! David was in self-preservation mode.*	✓
8. Had Uriah been aware of David's heart, would he have protected himself from David? – *Absolutely! Uriah had no idea he was being played like a fiddle.*	✓
9. Was David willing to burn at least one relational bridge over this? – *Absolutely! David was willing to go beyond duping Uriah—he called for his murder.*	✓
10. The idea of walking away from this potential fight and postponing the discussion or actions until another time didn't enter David's mind. – *Correct! Even when David inquired about Bathsheba as she bathed, he could have turned his back on his lust once he discovered she was married to Uriah, but he didn't.*	✓

Here we see that at the outset of these events, David could have chosen to not take Bathsheba to his bedroom. He could have assessed his reactions to determine whether he was in the flesh and then made different decisions.

Similarly, when we are at the initial stages of a potential church hurt, we have the opportunity to go through the checklist to determine whether our flesh is in control or not. Certainly, very few of us will walk around with a Church Hurt Checklist in our pockets, but one or two of these questions is really enough to jar you into awareness and perhaps thwart a divisive outcome.

For me, simply assessing my emotions and determining whether my response could burn a bridge is enough to at least cause me to stop and think about where the conflict could end up—either in the gutter or in godliness. And I haven't always been successful. Developing any new habit takes time and effort. And dealing with church hurts is not something most people face on a daily basis. So, it could be months or years between opportunities for practice. Nevertheless, start on smaller issues or practice on situations outside the church.

A friend once shared with me that he had had a major problem with road rage. If someone cut him off, he'd chase the offending driver for miles until he had the chance to confront him or her about what had happened. He said he knew he was out of control when he took a crow bar out against another driver. Thankfully, my friend got a hold of himself in time and there was no bloodshed. But, imagine what would have occurred if he hadn't taken a step back before forging ahead based upon hot-headed emotions?

His family would have been destroyed, as he owns a very lucrative business and manages its day-to-day operations. He could have done jail time if he was convicted of aggravated assault, using the crowbar in an unlawful manner and more. And, because he's a Christian, what kind of testimony would that have been for him, as someone who had led other men and women in various ministry roles?

Unfortunately, because of the sin nature of man—our flesh—we may not be able to go through life without ever encountering a church hurt. But we can see one approaching and decide to take a different route than what our flesh dictates.

Let's end this chapter by looking again at Romans 7.

> 17-20 But I need something more! For if I know the law
> but still can't keep it, and if the power of sin within me
> keeps sabotaging my best intentions, I obviously need help!
> I realize that I don't have what it takes. I can will it, but I
> can't do it. I decide to do good, but I don't really do it; I
> decide not to do bad, but then I do it anyway. My decisions,
> such as they are, don't result in actions. Something has gone
> wrong deep within me and gets the better of me every time.
>
> 21-23 It happens so regularly that it's predictable. The
> moment I decide to do good, sin is there to trip me up. I
> truly delight in God's commands, but it's pretty obvious
> that not all of me joins in that delight. Parts of me covertly
> rebel, and just when I least expect it, they take charge.
>
> 24 I've tried everything and nothing helps. I'm at the end
> of my rope. Is there no one who can do anything for me?
> Isn't that the real question?
>
> 25 The answer, thank God, is that Jesus Christ can and does.
> He acted to set things right in this life of contradictions
> where I want to serve God with all my heart and mind, but
> am pulled by the influence of sin to do something totally
> different.

In verses 17-25, Paul acknowledges the power of sin within us that continues to sabotage our best intentions. In *The Message* version of the Bible from which these verses are taken, Paul says that the sin nature rises up so regularly that it's predictable. And, because we're so often oblivious that the flesh is fueling our responses, we actually think that we're right in our statements and actions leading up to a church hurt.

Here, Paul says it so accurately when he states, "Parts of me covertly rebel, and just when I least expect it, they take charge." He's frustrated at losing this battle time and time again, until he finally acquiesces to the truth—that only Jesus Christ, our Lord, can do through us what we can't do through our flesh. That is, only He can empower us to be influenced by the Holy Spirit instead of succumbing to the flesh.

How does Christ do this? How is this achieved? It happens as we yield ourselves to Him and refrain from yielding to the flesh. I find that the more time I spend in prayer, fasting, reading the Word and in worship the easier it is for me to be yielded to Christ. And the yielding is a beautiful exchange in which I end up gaining so much more than what I give away. Being in His presence is transforming—turning my gloom and doom into warmth and sunshine and my weakness into strength. As I yield my time to Him, my heart, my thoughts and my actions follow.

Let me encourage you to not view this gentle instruction as another thing to put on your Christianity "To-Do List." Rather, I want you to view spending time with Jesus as taking a vacation from the flesh and from the minefield of volatile fruit the flesh produces. Run to Jesus as the writer of Hebrews admonishes us in chapter 12:2-4.

> ...let us lay aside every weight, and the sin which so easily ensnares us, and let us run with endurance the race that is set before us, 2 looking unto Jesus, the author and finisher of our faith, who for the joy that was set before Him endured the cross, despising the shame, and has sat down at the right hand of the throne of God. 3 For consider Him who endured such hostility from sinners against Himself, lest you become weary and discouraged in your souls. 4 You have not yet resisted to bloodshed, striving against sin.

And as you run to Him, know that He already paid the price for every flesh-driven disappointment and hurt you'll ever experience. He paid for the person who hurt you to be forgiven and He did it with His own blood. Similarly, He paid the price for the actions of your flesh, too.

CHAPTER 3

THE WORLD

When believers use the term "the world" it means those attitudes, behaviors, laws, values and beliefs that are spiritually unprofitable based on Scripture. The world is more than a place—it's a mindset shaped by societal trends, practices and beliefs, as opposed to a mindset shaped by biblical principles.

It may be tough to admit, but the world or worldly attitudes, practices and mindsets can follow born again Christians, like a gloomy shadow, right into the church. While worldliness is not an attractive characteristic, it is a deceptive one that can disguise itself as the norm when no prescribed rule exists to ensure that everyone is on the same page when it comes to treating each other in a manner that represents God.

The focus is often on clothing and lifestyle choices when believers discuss worldliness. Rarely is there a major discussion upholding God's view of bad behavior amongst Christians—be they co-workers, neighbors, friends, family or church family. Yet, I believe that worldliness regularly rears its ugly head in these relationships with immunity.

When I was a teenager, I considered myself a Christian, but had no idea of what the gospel message was all about. I had not invited Christ to become my personal Savior at that point, but my boyfriend's mother was a believer. She told me that as she was growing up, the definition of "worldly" constituted things like wearing red nail polish and lipstick, short dresses and even touching a deck of playing cards. And she explained that any type of dancing outside of shouting—Holy Spirit-fueled jubilance—was considered "worldly." Although she had shed most of those beliefs by the time I met her, my then-boyfriend's mother continued to uphold some rather strict guidelines to living holy and was intentional about ensuring that her son and I complied.

Recently, I watched the show, *Breaking Amish,* and I found that some of the things the Amish consider to be worldly are quite extreme when held up against the light of my personal choices. Women wearing makeup, showing their arms and letting down their hair are thought to be worldly behaviors to this group based on the little I learned from watching the reality show.

In fact, on the most recent episode I watched, a young woman desperately wanted to shed her Amish attire and begin wearing the "English" style clothing that most mainstream young Americans wear. Her two friends, a young man and a young woman, had previously broken from their Amish tradition and found freedom in wearing jeans, T-shirts, shorts and mini-skirts. But this young woman wanted more. She had visions of becoming a *fashionista*. She wanted her new attire to be even edgier than theirs had become. She wanted to blend shock value into her newfound style. Her friends, who felt that they were in the know concerning the "English" styles they were now sporting, were deeply offended that she was viewing them as not quite worldly enough, although she was brand new to their non-traditional lifestyle.

Here we can discern that worldliness or worldview can vary radically from group to group and from person to person. However, there are some general practices among mainline Christians that define our worldview.

Del Tackett of www.Focusonthefamily.com, defines a biblical worldview as being "…based on the infallible Word of God." Tackett adds, "When you believe the Bible is entirely true, then you allow it to be the foundation of everything you say and do. That means, for instance, you take seriously the mandate in Romans 13 to honor the governing authorities by researching the candidates and issues, making voting a priority."[2]

Thus, having a biblical worldview versus a worldly perspective are polar opposites. So, when it comes to church hurts, how does the world come into play? It does so in a similar fashion as with the flesh.

As the saying goes, Christians are *in* the world, but not *of* the world. But our living in the world means we are susceptible to the world's influences. One of the world's influences that often ignites church hurts include the need to win.

One of my guilty pleasures is watching the TV show *The Apprentice*. It is a quasi-reality show that pits groups of business people against each other in competition for a job working with real estate mogul Donald Trump.

The world's need to win is overtly highlighted on the show. Each week, one group of business people wins at a task for which they competed against the other group. Contestants on the losing team quickly betray their own team members when it comes to swaying Mr. Trump's decision about which member will be fired at the end of the show. The need to win becomes so vicious that the conference room is transformed into a feeding frenzy in which the weakest link is sacrificed as the others fight to keep their positions on the show alive.

This snapshot of the world's need to win bears down on believers as it represents what often goes on in the workplace where we spend a significant portion of each weekday. The bullying, the half-truths, the deflecting of responsibility, the cheating to get one leg up over the next guy are sometimes played out in our 9-to-5 lives. And sadly, this survival of the fittest mentality spills over into our lives at church.

For those fortunate enough to have grown up in the church, the world's influence on good church folk is no surprise. I've heard

2 http://www.focusonthefamily.com/faith/christian_worldview/whats_a_christian_worldview.aspx

stories from friends whose parents raised them in the church about affairs between married people, pastors engaging in inappropriate relationships with church members, and more. And although I wasn't raised in church, as an adult I learned of an incident in which a group of female teens, many of whom had parents deeply entrenched in ministry, decided to cause a younger group of girls to explore sex.

The conspiracy was to invite the younger girls to parties given by the older girls and encourage them to try things that the older girls had already tried. The plan included making the younger girls feel like they would be perceived as edgy and irreverent toward their parents' beliefs by taking on this new challenge.

My own daughter was one of the younger girls at the church during that time. When I ignorantly encouraged her to attend the party, she objected, sensing something was off with the older girls' sudden interest in her. Thankfully, she shut down my constant, sing-song barrage of "Aw...you should go," and "Oh...I think it's so nice that they want you to hang out with them." When I finally learned about what was going on, I was shocked that this group of church girls was willing to permanently damage younger girls for the sheer entertainment value of it all. And behind it all was the world's influence.

Because we are in the world, there is an ever-present pull, like the pull of gravity, to be like the world. Let's face it, as humans we want to be in the know concerning the world's trends and styles. We don't want to be left out of the latest fashion updates, hairstyles, technological changes or even cultural changes in behavior.

There was a time in American history when women were not welcome in business board rooms and as leaders of industry. That trend has changed radically. Recently, Mary Barra became the first female chief executive officer of a major American automaker, General Motors. This is something that was unheard of fifty years ago. Thus, the role of women in the business world has progressed significantly and the behavior of all business people towards women as leaders will be affected by these changes. And as behavioral changes in the world occur, those changes have an impact on the church as well.

So, how do we overcome the world's influence? The answer once again is through Jesus Christ. We overcome the world in its ability to influence us towards harming others and engaging in church hurts by patterning our lives after the Savior. In John 16:33 (NIV), we read:

> In the world you will have tribulation; but be of good cheer,
> I have overcome the world."

Here we read that Jesus has overcome the world. That means He overcame the world's influence over His life and His decisions. Jesus was intent on doing the Father's will. He came to earth with a purpose of dying for the sins of mankind—of being the atonement for the world's sins.

By simply following Christ's example, we too can overcome the world's influence and temptations. Think about what happened when Jesus was tempted by the devil in Matthew 4. His weapon for overcoming the temptations Satan put before Him was the word of God itself.

Let's take a look at the exchange to get a clear model from Jesus of how we are to overcome the world and its temptations:

> Then Jesus was led up by the Spirit into the wilderness to be tempted by the devil. 2 And when He had fasted forty days and forty nights, afterward He was hungry. 3 Now when the tempter came to Him, he said, "If You are the Son of God, command that these stones become bread."

> 4 But He answered and said, "It is written, 'Man shall not live by bread alone, but by every word that proceeds from the mouth of God.'"

> 5 Then the devil took Him up into the holy city, set Him on the pinnacle of the temple, 6 and said to Him, "If You are the

Son of God, throw Yourself down. For it is written: 'He shall give His angels charge over you,' and, 'In their hands they shall bear you up, Lest you dash your foot against a stone.'"

7 Jesus said to him, "It is written again, 'You shall not tempt the Lord your God.'" 8 Again, the devil took Him up on an exceedingly high mountain, and showed Him all the kingdoms of the world and their glory. 9 And he said to Him, "All these things I will give You if You will fall down and worship me."

10 Then Jesus said to him, "Away with you,[d] Satan! For it is written, 'You shall worship the Lord your God, and Him only you shall serve.'" 11 Then the devil left Him, and behold, angels came and ministered to Him.

Each time the devil put one of the world's influences in front of Jesus, He refuted it with the word of God. Similarly, the word becomes a weapon against the temptations that Satan dangles in front of you and me when we're in the throes of a brewing church hurt. Rather than maintaining our focus on the purpose of God the way that Jesus did, we often take Satan's bait and fall headlong into the abyss of a church hurt.

Let's look at what Satan said to Jesus and interpret these words through the language of a church hurt. Throughout this portion of Scripture, Satan cunningly raised the question, "If you are…" This is a temptation that he wields against us whenever we're about to embark on a church hurt. Satan's intention is to manipulate your self-esteem by throwing into question and causing you to grandstand about who God has called you to be—a child of God, like Jesus.

The purpose of this kind of temptation is to get you to exercise your spiritual authority on Satan's terms. He tempts you with the idea that "if you are" to be respected, you need to do something, like acting outside of the character of God, to make that happen. And "if you are" to be someone to be reverenced and reckoned with, you need to use whatever power you have to ensure that others recognize you as such.

Falling prey to these worldly aspirations can inflame church hurts when conflicts arise. The enemy—the god of this world—doesn't want you to focus on God's purpose for your life in the time of conflict. Remember how the enemy tried to distract Nehemiah as he was working to rebuild the walls of Jerusalem? Let's look at how he addressed this issue in Nehemiah 6:1-9.

> Now it happened when Sanballat, Tobiah, Geshem the Arab, and the rest of our enemies heard that I had rebuilt the wall, and that there were no breaks left in it (though at that time I had not hung the doors in the gates), 2 that Sanballat and Geshem sent to me, saying, "Come, let us meet together among the villages in the plain of Ono." But they thought to do me harm.
>
> 3 So I sent messengers to them, saying, "I am doing a great work, so that I cannot come down. Why should the work cease while I leave it and go down to you?"
>
> 4 But they sent me this message four times, and I answered them in the same manner.
>
> 5 Then Sanballat sent his servant to me as before, the fifth time, with an open letter in his hand. 6 In it was written: It is reported among the nations, and Geshem[a] says, that you and the Jews plan to rebel; therefore, according to these rumors, you are rebuilding the wall, that you may be their king. 7 And you have also appointed prophets to proclaim concerning you at Jerusalem, saying, "There is a king in Judah!" Now these matters will be reported to the king. So come, therefore, and let us consult together.
>
> 8 Then I sent to him, saying, "No such things as you say are being done, but you invent them in your own heart."
>
> 9 For they all were trying to make us afraid, saying, "Their hands will be weakened in the work, and it will not be done."
>
> Now therefore, O God, strengthen my hands.

Nehemiah had a burden to rebuild the broken down walls and gates of Jerusalem. He had heard from men of Judah that the city was burned down and that those inhabitants who had not been led into slavery after the Babylonian captivity were desolate. When Nehemiah heard of the state of Jerusalem and the people of God, he wept, prayed and fasted.

He was a slave himself—a cupbearer to the Persian King Artaxerxes. The Lord touched the king's heart and he granted Nehemiah permission to go and rebuild the walls. The king even gave Nehemiah letters that would allow him to pass through other areas in the region along the way to Jerusalem and to be given wood for the rebuilding.

As he progressed in the building project, there were those who opposed Nehemiah. Let's see what happened in Nehemiah 4:7.

> Now it happened, when Sanballat, Tobiah, the Arabs, the Ammonites, and the Ashdodites heard that the walls of Jerusalem were being restored and the gaps were beginning to be closed, that they became very angry, 8 and all of them conspired together to come and attack Jerusalem and create confusion. 9 Nevertheless we made our prayer to our God, and because of them we set a watch against them day and night.

Here we see that men who did not have the interests of God's kingdom at heart—representing the world—conspired together to attack Jerusalem and create confusion.

Are you are serving the Lord in the gifting that He has given you and within the purpose He has called you to? If so, expect the world's influence to come and attack you. The aim is to cause confusion within the kingdom of God and among its people. As such, instead of allowing this attack to drive a wedge of division between you and other believers through a church hurt, join forces with mature, trusted members of the body of Christ and pray. Follow Nehemiah's example and set a watch against them day and night.

What does setting a watch mean? It means being prepared for the enemy to show up to create confusion and division. As believers we can put a prayer shield around our church family and the relationships involved. But it's important to not wait until problems arise. Rather, set a watch during peaceful times—when there are no upsets and a church hurt hasn't set in.

At one time in my former ministry, I was part of a group called the "F.B.I.," or the Faithful Body of Intercessors. We prayed daily on behalf of the church, its members and the issues that could go wrong. We were setting a watch to keep the relational and spiritual walls of the church secure.

In order to avoid church hurts, it's important to acknowledge the world's influence in the church and that church people can hurt each other. This way, setting a watch is specifically targeted to appropriate areas of vulnerability.

In Nehemiah's case, he set a watch with half of the workers building the wall and the other half holding weapons to protect the wall. Nehemiah was clear that his purpose in rebuilding the wall was so important that it needed to be safeguarded. Similarly, the mission of the Church—to make disciples of all people—should not be left unprotected from the world's influence.

If you, like me, agree that church hurts destroy relationships and stunt the spiritual growth of the people involved, I encourage you to share with others that the world's influence is deeply rooted in church hurts. I also encourage you to note that being worldly, based on the clothing you wear or the trends you embrace, is far less problematic than taking on the world's influence regarding winning at all costs and looking good at the expense of others. Finally, I invite you to be open about the prospect of church hurts—even among well-meaning Christians—and to set a watch around those you walk with in ministry.

CHAPTER 4

THE DEVIL

Many years ago, a comedian named Flip Wilson—one of the first African American men to host his own variety TV show in the 1970s—regularly portrayed a female character named Geraldine Jones. This character was known for using a signature line whenever she had done something wrong. Geraldine would simply say, "The devil made me do it!" Geraldine blamed the devil for everything from her reckless driving and overspending to her torrid love life with her boyfriend, Killer.

This chapter is not aimed at blaming church hurts exclusively on the devil, but to help us to see our vulnerability when it comes to Satan's schemes in leveraging divisions to cause greater relational break-downs in the church. Think about it, what does the devil have to gain from a church hurt? How does the enemy benefit from believers who don't walk together in unity?

First of all, the Scriptures help us to understand that there is power in agreement. In Matthew 18:19-20, Jesus explains this, saying:

> "Again I say to you that if two of you agree on earth concerning anything that they ask, it will be done for them by My Father in heaven. 20 For where two or three are gathered together in My name, I am there in the midst of them."

Here we have a conditional promise from Jesus that requires us to be in agreement in order to obtain anything we ask. Thus, if we pray together about a situation and we are in agreement, God will move on our behalf. But Satan doesn't want this. Let's say there is a high crime area in a particular community and young people are engaging in drug dealing and violence. Does this advance the kingdom of God or the devil's plans for humanity?

Certainly, the devil wants to see human life destroyed. He is jealous of God's love for mankind and mankind's love for God. He wants to steal that love, and he will use whatever means necessary to get it—even taking away young people's chances of coming to faith in Jesus Christ by killing them at a young age.

You may be thinking, *'It's not the devil. It's the criminal element out there. If young people would just stay in school and not get involved in crime, they would avoid violence and jail.'* I beg to differ. I believe it is the devil's plan to divert people—both young and old—away from the things of God by leading them towards destruction. Isn't that what happened in the Garden to Eve?

Shiny Object Syndrome

One of Satan's tactics is one I call *Shiny Object Syndrome*. That means he holds up something that catches the eye. And, like a street peddler, he tells us all the attributes of this object—how good it is, how much it will do for us. Then, when we take it, we discover that it's a trap.

That's what happened to Eve. She was beguiled by the serpent in the Garden by Shiny Object Syndrome. Let's read the account in Genesis 3:1-7.

> Now the serpent was more cunning than any beast of the field which the Lord God had made. And he said to the woman, "Has God indeed said, 'You shall not eat of every tree of the garden'?"
>
> 2 And the woman said to the serpent, "We may eat the fruit of the trees of the garden; 3 but of the fruit of the tree

which is in the midst of the garden, God has said, 'You shall not eat it, nor shall you touch it, lest you die.'"

4 Then the serpent said to the woman, "You will not surely die. 5 For God knows that in the day you eat of it your eyes will be opened, and you will be like God, knowing good and evil."

6 So when the woman saw that the tree was good for food, that it was pleasant to the eyes, and a tree desirable to make one wise, she took of its fruit and ate. She also gave to her husband with her, and he ate. 7 Then the eyes of both of them were opened, and they knew that they were naked; and they sewed fig leaves together and made themselves coverings.

What was the shiny object the serpent held up before Eve? It was the "forbidden fruit." He pointed to the very thing God said she shouldn't eat and made it seem so appealing that she gave in and disobeyed God. He broke it down by telling her that she wouldn't die, that God knew that her eyes would be opened, and that she would be like God, knowing good and evil. Eve went and checked out the tree bearing the fruit God said to not eat from. She agreed with Satan that it was pleasant to the eyes and a tree desirable to make one wise. Then, she ate the fruit. Next, she gave some to her husband, Adam, and he ate it, too.

Eve fell into the trap of Shiny Object Syndrome. First, she listened to the devil and compared what he was saying to what God had said. In the comparison, she weighed what Satan said, "For God knows that in the day you eat of it your eyes will be opened, and you will be like God, knowing good and evil." He appealed to Eve based on what she didn't have—the knowledge of good and evil. He led her to believe that this was a disadvantage and that she would be like God if she had it.

What did Satan have to gain from using Shiny Object Syndrome to cause Adam and Eve to sin? He knew that they would lose their place of security in God and become open prey for his schemes. Remember that the enemy himself had lost his place in the kingdom of God, too. Let's read an excerpt from Sharefaith.com that describes what happened when Satan, the former archangel named Lucifer, lost his position in God's kingdom.

Lucifer is one of three archangels mentioned in Scripture. He was created by God just as all angels were, but his role was different from the other angelic hosts. Lucifer was referred to as the 'covering angel.' Just as the cherubim covered the mercy seat of the Ark of the Covenant, Lucifer was established by God to be the angel of worship, one whose ministry surrounded the heart of heaven. Lucifer was created to dwell eternally in the throne room of heaven, in the very presence of God (Ezekiel 28:14).

Lucifer had wisdom, beauty, ability, perfection, and yet he wanted more; he wanted to be worshiped like God. But God does not share His glory, nor does He permit another to receive worship. So before Lucifer had a chance to make his move, he was removed from the presence of God. Cast out of heaven like a bolt of lightning, Lucifer was stripped of his beauty, his position, and his rights to heaven. Satan's constant attempt ever since has been to oppose the mighty plan of God. He even attempted to tempt Jesus to sin and worship him.

Lucifer's name, 'son of the morning,' was given to a far more deserving individual, the Son of God. Jesus Christ is called the 'Bright and Morning Star' (Revelation 22:16). Today, Jesus is seated at the right hand of God, dwelling in the presence of the Almighty. Christ's words hold true, even in the account of Satan: "Whoever exalts himself will be humbled, and he who humbles himself will be exalted" (Matthew 23:12).

So, from this article—which is based upon Scripture—we can see that Satan had once held a place in God's presence. And after losing that position, he wanted to steal man's connection with God so that he could beguile man to worship him. It's important to know that Satan wants to win at any cost. He's willing to distract people away from God so that he can trick them into serving him.

Getting back to what goes on in crime-ridden communities, serving Satan can come in the form of getting young people hooked on drugs, causing them to rob or burglarize for drug money and ruining their ability to live out God's purpose for their lives.

If believers are in agreement that we want to stop Satan's plan in our communities, we can come together to pray—touching and agreeing based upon Matthew 18:19—and receive God's promise, which says He will do the very thing we ask. Thus, if we are in agreement, we will ask that God deliver the drug dealers, cause them to come to a saving knowledge of Jesus Christ and then use them to lead others Christ. If we are in agreement, we will pray that those who have become drug addicted get free and come to a place of wholeness physically, mentally, emotionally and spiritually. If we are in agreement, we will also pray for the restoration of our community—that it becomes a place where businesses can thrive, where children can play and where people can walk the streets without fear of being robbed or harassed.

But Satan doesn't want us to pray in agreement. It benefits him greatly if we are at odds with one another because we won't come together in agreement, and society will stay just as he wants it—filled with people vulnerable to his tricks and tactics.

When it comes to church hurts, Satan uses the issues surrounding the hurt to perpetuate his Shiny Object Syndrome. Like he did with Eve, he will hold up the offense you may have experienced with your brother or sister in Christ and say something like, *'Are you going to let him/her get away with that? That wasn't right! You need to tell that person off. Or better yet, you need to tell your friends about it so that they will be warned about that person, too!'*

And although Satan approached Eve in the Garden, during your church hurt, he will speak to you in the area of your emotions. Remember what got Satan removed from the presence of God? It was pride. And when you start agreeing with him, the way that Eve did, you're agreeing in that area of your emotions called pride.

What does the Bible say about pride? We find the answer in Proverbs 16:18, which reads:

> Pride goes before destruction, and a haughty spirit before a fall.

See, Satan doesn't want you to agree with your brothers and sisters in Christ to effect change in your community, in your region and in the world. No, he wants you to get in agreement with *him* and become prideful regarding some petty offense that he can blow up and cause you and other believers to not come together to win souls for the kingdom of God.

Pride

While we know that pride comes before a fall, what's so wrong with it? How does Satan use pride in church hurts to intensify a small problem and make it into a bigger one? We just read why he does it—to get people not to agree because agreement facilitates answered prayers. But let's look at how he leverages pride to affect divisions in the church.

What is pride? From a spiritual standpoint, pride is self-promotion, self-righteousness and self-preservation. This is my definition and, to break it down further, it means that we are in pride when we want to beat a drum touting ourselves as having greater abilities, looks, intellect or righteousness than others. It also means we are willing to preserve our egos—looking good before others—at all costs. Pride says, *'I am doing this right, and you're doing this wrong. I am right, and you are wrong. I am the right person for the job, and you are the wrong person. My opinion is the right one, and yours is the wrong one.'*

Here we see a pattern that shows that when we are in a prideful state, we are all about being right or better in some way than someone else, and we are all about making that person wrong. When it comes to church hurts, the devil uses this kind of pride to drive wedges between people.

Again, the way a church hurt progresses is that something happens. There is a beginning to the event of a church hurt. Whatever that issue is, there is an opportunity for the people involved to not get into pride, but to humble themselves one to another, forgive the offense and move forward. Sadly, that doesn't often happen. What typically does happen is that the people involved move into self-promotion, self-righteousness or self-preservations and the issue becomes magnified. And, as the Bible says in Galatians 5:9, "A little leaven leavens the whole lump."

In cooking, leaven is a substance used to expand dough to make it rise. If you eat a cracker, there's a lot of crunch to it because not much leavening, if any at all, was used in the dough. Why? This is because if we want crackers, we need dough that's flat and dry. On the other hand, if we want the end product to be soft and fluffy, like some breads or doughnuts, we want the dough to have lots of air in it. So, we add leavening agents, like baker's yeast, to add gas to the dough. This makes the dough rise and the bread that is produced has holes in it when you look at the inside of it.

When it comes to church hurts, pride is a leavening agent to the actual issue that occurred. Let's say, for example, that you had been the person singing in the lead in your church's worship team. One morning, you get a flat tire, and you're late. There's no way you can make it to church on time to lead worship. Once you arrive, you find that Jewel, another member of the worship team, was asked to lead in your place. She does so and you're happy that the worship went forward, until they ask Jewel to lead worship again and there is no flat tire on your part.

The pastor and music director seem to like Jewel's worship leading just as well as yours. Now, there's a problem. You suddenly find fault with Jewel. She doesn't sing on key. She wears the wrong clothing. Her children are misbehaved. You find yourself sharing these thoughts with others. Soon, there are a few of you who agree that Jewel is just not right for the role of worship leader. Sure, she's okay in a pinch, but there's just too much wrong with her to have her leading worship regularly. Before you know it, there's an altercation between you and Jewel. Those who agreed with you that there was too much wrong with Jewel for her to be worship leader are on your side. Those who agree with Jewel that she's been picked on are on her side. The sound of worship has changed in the church. Now it's tainted by jealousy, offenses and pride.

Do you see how pride is the leavening agent in a church hurt? It's the very thing that was introduced at the beginning of the event that caused the "problem" to rise like yeast causes dough to rise. But what actually was the problem in the first place? There was no precedent set for sharing the position of worship leader. While the church cannot be held responsible for preparing for every potential outcome, there could have been a conversation as the worship teams were being developed that set the tone for sharing the role of worship leader. This way, no one could take a prideful "ownership" of the position. Regardless, the responsibility is mine and yours to note when pride is creeping into our lives. Pride is the number one tool of the devil when it comes to perpetuating church hurts. Further, pride is the first thing in the list of seven things God hates in Proverbs 6:16-19.

> These six *things* the Lord hates,
> Yes, seven *are* an abomination to Him:
> 17 A proud look,
> A lying tongue,
> Hands that shed innocent blood,
> 18 A heart that devises wicked plans,
> Feet that are swift in running to evil,

19 A false witness *who* speaks lies,
And one who sows discord among brethren.

Humility

The opposite of pride is humility, and it can be used to defuse church hurts when we see them arising. In the face of a church hurt, humility looks like someone who is acquiescing to another to avoid a relationship breakdown.

There is often a battle between pride and humility, though. It doesn't take as much effort to allow humility to win as it does to uphold pride, however. Whenever we walk in humility, it's like dropping a heavy weight off of our backs.

Imagine walking up ten flights of stairs wearing a backpack weighed down with 50 lbs. of bricks. By the time you reached the third flight of stairs, you'd probably be more than happy to let go of the excess weight. Taking it off, setting it down and continuing up the stairs would make your life so much easier in this situation. That's how it is with humility. When you simply let go of the pride—thereby letting go of the leavening agent that makes a problem worse—you can freely walk in humility.

My definition of humility is self-less love. It is caring for others as I care for myself. That means, if I'm wrong, I embrace a willingness to admit my wrong to the person I harmed, ask their forgiveness and repent by not repeating the behavior.

Humility is easier said than done, though, because pride is standing there, with the devil as its cheerleader, telling me that I shouldn't let the other person get away with the offense that is threatening our relationship. Again, my agreement with the devil will cause me to lean in pride's direction. *'Yeah, that person did me wrong. Who does she think she's dealing with? My parents didn't raise me to be a punk!'*

But humility speaks the words of Psalm 133, which tells us how God feels when we walk together in unity.

> Behold, how good and how pleasant it is for brethren to dwell together in unity!
>
> 2 It is like the precious oil upon the head, running down on the beard,
> the beard of Aaron, running down on the edge of his garments.
> 3 It is like the dew of Hermon, descending upon the mountains of Zion;
> for there the Lord commanded the blessing—life forevermore·

This psalm is filled with imagery that depicts God's delight in the unity of his people. In Matthew Henry's commentary on Psalm 133, he explains the symbolism this way:

> "[Unity] is fragrant as the holy anointing oil, which was strongly perfumed, and diffused its odours, to the great delight of all the bystanders, when it was poured upon the head of Aaron, or his successor the high priest, so plentifully that it ran down the face, even to the collar or binding of the garment.
>
> It was very precious, and the like to it was not to be made for any common use. Thus holy love is, in the sight of God, of great price; and that is precious indeed which is so in God's sight.
>
> It is fructifying. It is profitable as well as pleasing; it is as the dew; it brings abundance of blessings along with it, as numerous as the drops of dew. It cools the scorching heat of men's passions, as the evening dews cool the air and refresh the earth. It contributes very much to our fruitfulness in everything that is good; it moistens the heart, and makes it

tender and fit to receive the good seed of the word; as, on the contrary, malice and bitterness unfit us to receive it.[3]

So, although this is a brief psalm, of only three verses, we can see from the commentary exposition that it is power-packed with description regarding the significance of unity from God's perspective.

So, if we value what God values, our unity—leavened by humility—is something worth safeguarding and preserving. Further, it is something that the enemy wants to steal. Remember what Jesus said in John 10:10,

> The thief does not come except to steal, and to kill, and to destroy. I have come that they may have life, and that they may have it more abundantly.

Here, Jesus tells us what Satan is up to when it comes to mankind or anything else God loves. He comes to steal, kill and destroy it. Besides destroying relationships in God's kingdom, the enemy also wants to rob you of your faith. The Book of Hebrews declares that without faith it is impossible to please God, thus if the enemy can get you to give up your faith in the wake of a church hurt, you are no longer someone who can please God.

I invite you to acknowledge the devil's schemes in using church hurts to further his objective to isolate you so that you are less effective, so that you are not walking in agreement with other believers, so that you chase his shiny objects, including pride, and so that you are out of unity, humility and most importantly faith.

---

3 http://www.biblestudytools.com/commentaries/matthew-henry-complete/psalms/133.html

CHAPTER 5

WHY DOES IT HURT SO BAD?

What differentiates church hurts from other types of hurts is the fact that we often give so much of ourselves to our roles and relationships at church. It's a place where we interact with our colleagues on a basis of at least once or twice a week, and we do so based upon an agreed assumption of integrity and honor.

Church-based relationships typically function based upon some semblance of biblical standards of conduct. Unfortunately, there's often a slippery slope when it comes to biblical standards of conduct in today's churches. No disrespect to your church, which I'm sure operates purely based upon Scriptural standards, it's the church across town that—wink, wink—needs help.

The Haves and The Have-Nots

When the church across town deals with issues that come up between people, often there are different standards for different people. No one likes to admit it, but there are times when the person who is a big giver at the church is dealt with differently than the guy who isn't such a great tither. Why? The reason is because some churches rely heavily on that person who is a big giver to keep the lights on.

While we'd like to believe that the church world is made up of the mega churches we see on television, according to The Barna group, the average Protestant church size in America is 89 adults. And 60 percent of protestant churches have less than 100 adults in attendance. Only 2 percent have over 1000 adults attending.[4] Thus, when a church hurt occurs, a less than completely biblical solution may be applied based primarily on economics. Other issues affecting the equity of church hurt solutions are also family relationships and personality/popularity dynamics.

These issues make church hurts a bit more emotionally challenging because of the inequities they pose for one side of the conflict. Because we expect justice and equity to be upheld at church, when it is not, the offense is exponentially greater.

A Safe Place?

Another reason why church hurts are so damaging is because church is supposed to be a safe place. I didn't grow up in the church, so I didn't know, like some of my church family members, that I should be on guard. After my salvation experience, I believed that God's people were trustworthy, even-handed and morally bound to treating each other according to what we call The Golden Rule. This rule, found in Matthew 7:12, tells us to do unto others as you would have others do unto you. It means that we should treat other people the way we want to be treated. Sounds simple enough, right? Wrong. We each have different standards for how we treat other people in comparison to how we treat ourselves.

Although I expected the church to be a place where the Golden Rule was upheld, that wasn't always the case. I even heard of a situation in which someone who depended on the church for his employment visa was nearly deported because a spiteful leader at the church held back the documents needed to secure is ongoing residency in the United States. He and his wife could have been deported within weeks had someone on staff not alerted the guy about what the leader was up to. And I am certain that the leader would have not been happy if the shoe were on the other foot and he was within

---

4 http://careynieuwhof.com/2013/09/8-reasons-most-churches-never-break-the-
   200-attendance-mark/

weeks of being deported because someone in the household of faith deliberately withheld the signing of the necessary papers. But, the Golden Rule wasn't applied. Rather, a power play was being used to harm someone simply because this leader had the power to do so. The safety that that unsuspecting church worker should have been able to rely upon was a complete façade.

So where do we get the idea that we're under an umbrella of safety within our churches? I believe it comes from the Church's perceived position in society. The church has been viewed as the place where we expect to be cared for in various ways—physically, spiritually, emotionally and relationally. Because God provides this type of care for us, it is often our expectation that the church, as His representative, will not do us any type of harm.

Sadly, there are so many cases of abuse in the church that it is simply not true that churches are safe places. As a former church staff member, I can attest that it was certainly our belief that we were offering a safe place of worship. Yet, people got hurt. As long as humans gather together, there will be conflict, challenges and potential hurts.

The shock that exacerbates the pain of a church hurt is borne out of the idea that we believed we were safe. We didn't think it would be a church person who would do something so egregious to us. We were completely vulnerable because we thought we could be.

I recall watching a television program that documented the life of a woman who spent a good part of her adult life in jail. What led up to her imprisonment was that she had sent her son to Christian camp one summer. While at the camp, the boy was sexually assaulted by a cook. That was bad enough, but the cook continued stalking the child after several court appearances. The mother, who had spent about five years changing her residence from place to place to keep the stalker at bay, was extremely stressed and frustrated with the criminal justice process. Unfortunately, she took the law into her own hands and shot the accused man one fateful day as he was exiting the courthouse. That mother went to jail and was unable to raise her son, who she had tried so desperately to protect.

Certainly, the crime of sexual assault can happen to a child at school or anywhere, but in this case and in many others, it happened at a Christian camp, which is representative of the Church. And when such acts—not simply emotional assaults, but criminal ones—occur in places of worship or places sanctioned by the Church, the pain reverberates throughout society.

The trust of the church is lessened by all forms of hurtful acts and the effect is that people are weary of putting their faith in God. The question arises as to whether the people in the church are truly serving God or serving themselves on behalf of the spiritual vulnerability of others.

Spiritual Vulnerability

I define spiritual vulnerability as that state of belief that accepts the rationales, explanations and excuses of church leaders based on their spiritual authority in our lives. That means that despite how we would process the same information in other settings, we acquiesce to church leaders because we view them as somehow more authoritative, knowledgeable or closer to God than we are. Therefore, we believe they must be telling us the truth or dealing with us based on righteousness. Sadly, this is not only spiritually dangerous, but dangerous in a myriad of ways.

Back in November 1978, 909 Americans were massacred at a South American church compound of the San Francisco-based religious organization known as The People's Temple. Led by Jim Jones, the church fostered racial integration, socialism and an unwavering allegiance to its causes and to Jones' decisions.

Jones ordered the mass suicide in the Guyanese jungle that he had converted into a church compound he called Jonestown.

Congregants included children, ranging from infants to teens, as well as senior adults and all ages in between. Further, members of The People's Temple were of all races. And although Jones had led several rehearsals involving the congregants drinking a fake poison, reports indicate that a large number of the dead willingly took the actual poison and gave it to their parents and children, ending their lives.

Survivors of the ordeal indicate that while at the compound people were starved, beaten and berated for any dissention. Still, some miraculously reached out to U.S. Congressman Leo Ryan of California for his help in getting rescued. The congressman toured the compound and led a group of people who indicated they wanted to leave to the airport. There, he and members of his press crew were shot and killed as they attempted to board a plane headed back to the United States with a group who said they were being held at the compound against their will.

It is likely that the killing of the congressman led Jones to call for the mass suicide. He had beguiled the congregants into believing that the cause of The People's Temple was worth not only dying for, but worth taking the lives of their parents and children for. Jones also died in the massacre, but it is undetermined if he committed suicide or was murdered during the incident.

Obviously, The People's Temple was a cult in its final years. And sadly, many people were not only hurt, but coerced into aiding and abetting the murder and suicide of hundreds of individuals and entire families.

Clearly, this "church" was not a safe place. The unadulterated loyalty that was required to rise up the ranks of the ministry and to be sanctioned as a dedicated member went beyond the pale of what makes sense to us in hindsight. But, those spiritually vulnerable souls that loss their lives most likely believed they were doing "God's will."

According to a report from ABC News, the church did many good deeds, but followers were never allowed to criticize Jones or talk to others outside the group. They signed contracts vowing their allegiance. "It was a cult, total mind control," said Leslie Wagner-Wilson, who, as a teen, traveled the country recruiting members. "The church would humiliate you and take away any ego you had. Everything centered on the cause," she said.

Laura Johnston Kohl, another Jonestown survivor, said, "There was no forum for us to do any kind of questioning on decisions Jim made. He was in charge. It was either Jim or his mistresses or secretaries who made decisions."[5]

Over 30 years later, survivors are still struggling with feelings of guilt and anguish about those they left behind and the fact that they were involved with such a radical organization. Wilson reported that she had three failed marriages, engaged in drug use, has had suicidal thoughts and is still weary of organized religion all these years later.

Where do you draw the line?

In considering the best approach to avoiding a church hurt that teeters between blind loyalty and personal safety, the question becomes where do you draw the line? At what point do you walk away while also maintaining a healthy faith in God, despite the representation of a rogue organization?

I believe the answer lies in what Jonestown survivor Leslie Wagner-Wilson said, "...the church would take away any ego you had. Everything centered on the cause."

Whenever your relationship with your church or its leaders compromises your personal sense of individuality and when you feel pressured to work for or attend to its vision, mission, programs and events beyond your own personal choice, I assert that you may not be in a safe place and could experience some level of hurt.

---

5 http://abcnews.go.com/Health/jonestown-massacre-anniversary-survivors-wrestle-guilt/story?id=17741732&page=2

My mother was a New York City police officer in the 1970s. She retired in the 1990s, at a time when I was legalistically loyal to the church I attended. Legalistic Christians are people who strictly adhere to lifestyle rules that distinguish them as born again. They dress very modestly, never drink or smoke, never gamble, rarely use profanity, and are always on the lookout for anything that would peg them as worldly or in the presence of demons. My choices at that time weren't all bad, but it certainly caused me to be somewhat judgmental of people who didn't follow the lifestyle that I followed.

During the time when she was a beat cop, my mother patrolled the streets of Harlem, where we were from. Back then, Harlem hadn't undergone its current gentrification. The streets were tough, especially at night. Drug dealers, dope fiends, robbers, pimps and a myriad of criminals were out doing whatever they do during the early morning hours. And my mother was out there, too, wearing what she affectionately called her Blue Bull's-Eye—her police uniform.

One day while we were talking she made a statement that stuck with me. My mother said, "You can always tell who the Christians are on the street at 2 a.m. when the bars close because they're the ones dragging their children behind them."

Compared to the Jamestown massacre, a family with children leaving a Harlem church at 2 a.m. is pretty benign. Yet, the idea that a police officer—someone used to assessing who's who on the streets, especially in the wee hours of the morning—would note that Christians are the ones who keep their sleepy children out as late as the bars and dance clubs close in New York City, was a piercing illustration to me.

I was a Christian parent at that time. I was at the church whenever the doors were opened. Early on, my kids did their homework on Wednesday nights at Children's Church. And if we were having a guest speaker or conference on a Friday night, we could easily be out way past their bedtimes—not until 2 a.m., but certainly way past their bedtimes.

But like the people my mother encountered, who kept their children out at all hours, we had a better cause than the drug dealers and pimps. We were ensuring that our children were in the presence of good, solid Bible teaching, worship, prayer and the like. Yet, it never dawned on me that someone who wasn't born again, and my mother was not a born-again believer at that time, would notice that we believers had a greater allegiance to being at church with our kids in the middle of the night than we had to making sure they were home in bed at a decent hour. And it wasn't that the parents she saw were consciously making unsafe choices for their children, but they certainly were setting a precedent for their children to be unable to make safety-oriented decisions for themselves when it came to pursuing their allegiance to the churches they'd eventually attend.

When a church hurt occurs, the memories of how much personal sacrifice you've made for the church comes to the fore. That's one reason why it hurts so badly. You've kept your kids out late at night, jeopardized your own personal safety, perhaps given money that was already ear-marked for personal bills, and maybe even taken time away from work to serve the church. And when a church hurt hits you, these sacrifices reverberate in your heart along with the feelings of anguish you may be experiencing due to the trauma of whatever has happened.

Time, Talent and Treasure

At my former church, we heard a lot of sermons involving giving our time, talent and treasure to the church. At the time I didn't believe that I was being manipulated, and I still don't. It's a good message. If you're a member of a church and you're enjoying the benefits of membership or of being a visitor for that matter, why not give back from your time, talent and treasure? It makes sense and it's fair to do so. But the problem arises when you give of your time, talent and treasure to the detriment of other obligations or when you go beyond the norm in giving and there is no reciprocal giving back to you. And, when faced with a church hurt, the giving of your time, talent and treasure feels very personally sacrificial and leaves you feeling as if you're owed something in return. In avoiding church hurts, I invite you to seek to strike a healthy balance in the giving of your time, talent and treasure.

One day I was out with a church colleague of mine at a fast food restaurant. When the pastor of our church came into the restaurant, we thought it was completely fortuitous. We'd be the ones with bragging rights for having had a Saturday afternoon hamburger with the pastor. But after greeting us, the pastor asked my friend to step aside so that they could speak privately. They exchanged something, he left and she returned to our table. When we left the restaurant, it was clear that the pastor had come to borrow her car since it was gone and his was left in its place.

At the time, my friend drove a nicer car than the pastor and he needed to attend an event and wanted to drive her car. Nothing wrong with that, I thought. Later, though, I learned that my friend was not only allowing the pastor to drive her car whenever he wanted to, but she was using her vacation time to baby-sit his children so that he and his wife could spend their vacation time away without their children.

"What about your vacation?" I asked her once.

"Oh, I don't mind," she said. "He's the pastor. He deserves to go on vacation more than I do," was her response.

I eventually left that church, so I can't tell you if my friend stayed around giving and giving to that pastor, but I do know that her family was very unhappy with the arrangement. My friend was giving her time, talent and treasure to the church through the pastor and exhibited a firm unwillingness to listen to me or to her parents about the choices she was making.

Because the pastor had hurt me—telling me that I needed to "work my way back to salvation" after I left the church because of his controlling spirit—my guess is that my friend was hurt, too. Let's assume for a moment that she was. What was the cost of her giving her time, talent and treasure? The cost was that she gave away some things that were intangible and there was little to no quid pro quo—or an equal return—for her giving.

Sure, he was the pastor and she was the congregant. There was a mutual give and take there as it should have been. But, he used his role as the pastor to gain certain advantages that he did not return to her. There was never a time when he offered to, say, paint her apartment in exchange for her using her vacation time to watch his kids or for using her vehicle.

Thus, if she, too, experienced a church hurt there, this unbalanced giving—which provided the pastor with special advantages based upon the relationship that she wasn't also afforded—the church hurt on her end was deeper. Why? It's because her investment was bigger than the agreed upon relationship of pastor and congregant.

And why did she give of her time, talent and treasure beyond the publicized needs of the church? Why do many of us church members do things for the pastor or other church leaders that they would never do for us in return? I believe that it's because we are seeking an advantage over others in the church. We want to be closer to the pastor than others in the congregation. We want to be "teacher's pet," so to speak. Now no self-respecting adult wants to admit that he or she is playing this game, but sadly, we do. Unfortunately, giving beyond the church's requirements, beyond wat's made public and beyond what's safe to give is another reason church hurts cut so deeply.

As you foster your church relationship, I encourage you to carefully consider your motives in giving of your loyalty, time, talent and treasure. Consider that it may not be safe for you to do so beyond certain limits. Also, remember that some church relations are based on greater financial ties, personality or family connections than you may be able to compete with. The bottom line is it's important that you protect yourself against the pain of church hurts or spend time learning to overcome them.

CHAPTER 6

OVERCOMING CHURCH HURTS

Back in the late 1990s, there was a bestselling book out titled, *Who Moved My Cheese?* The author, Dr. Spencer Johnson, wrote the book as an allegory of how we deal with change. Just as the title indicates, when something happens to change the norms we've become accustomed to, instead of quickly adapting to the change, we often stop and wonder, *'Who Moved My Cheese?'* In other words, we spend considerable time questioning why the change occurred rather than reacting to the change so that whatever is now missing in our lives can quickly be replaced.

In the book, two mice—Sniff and Scurry—rise up each morning and go to where they know they'll find the cheese they want. The cheese represents what they need in their lives to keep them alive, happy and well adjusted. Similarly, two Littlepeople—Hem and Haw—rise up each morning and go to the same place to gather their cheese for the day.

Sniff and Scurry, because they are mice, depend largely upon instinct. And they can sense that the cheese in the place where they had been going daily was dwindling. They were paying attention and were ready to move on once the cheese was completely gone. Not so for Hem and Haw. They had become so used to getting the cheese from the same location that it was hard for them to move forward. Instead of looking for cheese elsewhere, they hung back, wondering who in the world had moved their cheese. Although the question *should* have been, 'Hey, where can we find some more cheese?' instead, they spent their days stuck in the past. They were also afraid of leaving the comfort of where their cheese used to be. Even though it was now empty, they believed that at least they were guarding themselves against the fear of the unknown.

Sniff and Scurry had long since found a new place where cheese was plentiful before Haw finally got up the courage to venture out of the old spot in search of new cheese. Although he was afraid, he kept moving forward and writing sayings on the wall in case his friend, Hem, decided to follow. The sayings were things like, "What would you do if you weren't afraid?" and "Smell the cheese often so you know when it is getting old."

Eventually, Haw discovers a new cheese facility. It's the same one Sniff and Scurry had located earlier, but there was plenty cheese to go around. Haw was both proud and satisfied that he had gotten over the loss of the old familiar cheese dispensary and strapped up his sneakers to find a new one.

When a church hurt occurs in your life, not only is it painful and devastating to some of the important relationships you've built there, but it also can leave a huge hole in your lifestyle. Not only is the regularity of your schedule interrupted, but it's also likely that you simply don't trust people—especially so-called godly people—anymore. This is a huge change in that it is very likely that the church and the significant people involved in the hurt you're processing were major pillars in your entire faith experience.

The change presented by a church hurt is similar to the dilemma of Hem and Haw in *Who Moved My Cheese?* The cheese in the case of a church hurt represents the roles and relationships that will change because of the hurt. While I'm not suggesting that these roles and relationships have to end completely, they will and should change—for the better. Whatever initiated the church hurt and the words and actions that ensued should be examined with a heart toward forgiveness and repentance, thus affecting a positive change in the relationship.

Sadly, getting to the point of forgiveness and repentance often takes a lot longer than necessary after a church hurt. This is because when we're feeling hurt, we often hold on to the pain longer than necessary. Wouldn't it be great if we could simply let go of hurt feelings so that we could quickly get to the happiness we desire?

Letting it go

When something bad happens in our lives, like a church hurt, an important way to deal with it is to let it go. Believe it or not, holding on to the pain, to the story of what happened, to the residual fallout of the relational breakdown, is harder than letting it go.

But letting go without addressing the issue is not exactly what I mean here. Let's face it, not every infraction requires a formal sit down meeting with a counselor. There are some issues that can be let go of without much fanfare. However, when a church hurt occurs that is of a more serious nature, having a talk with the person or people who hurt you could be a wise approach. The Bible admonishes us in Matthew 18:15-17 on how to deal with such issues:

> 15 "If your brother or sister[b] sins,[c] go and point out their fault, just between the two of you. If they listen to you, you have won them over. 16 But if they will not listen, take one or two others along, so that 'every matter may be established by the testimony of two or three witnesses.'[d] 17 If they still refuse to listen, tell it to the church; and if they refuse to listen even to the church, treat them as you would a pagan or a tax collector.

Let's take a look at the instructions in this passage. First, it says, if your brother or sister sins against you, go to them *privately* and discuss it. Often, when dealing with a church hurt, we end up going to other people—people who are not involved—first and venting to them about what happened. That means that the person who gets the earful about the one who hurt you is left with an impression that will likely taint their view of that person.

Although it may seem natural and sensible to have a pre-discussion with someone else about the person who hurt you, the reality is that this step is simply gossip. When you plant a negative notion about someone into the psyche of another person, it is gossip, plain and simple. And the Book of Proverbs 26:20 tells us, *"Without wood a fire goes out; without a gossip a quarrel dies down."* Thus, if you want the church hurt to subside, don't engage in gossip. Instead, refer to the teaching in Matthew 18; go to the person responsible for hurting you and have a discussion about it.

You may wonder how you can have a productive conversation when anger and other unbridled emotions could take over and make matters worse. Well, I invite you to set up the conversation by sharing with the person who hurt you what you want the outcome to be. And, whatever you devise as an outcome should be a win-win for the both of you.

Aside from my academic studies in communications, I also took a course in interpersonal communication where we learned to "dance in the conversation." That is, we learned how to be less stiff-necked in our positions so that conversations, even difficult ones, can flow like a dance instead of a tug-of-war. We also learned that our words create a world. This means that if you want the outcome to be one of love and forgiveness, choose words that reflect love and forgiveness.

Apply these pointers when you converse with the person who hurt you. Choose your words carefully and don't be dogmatic about your position. Remember that the other person has a point of view, too. Don't start off by telling them how what they did made you feel. If you're really committed to strengthening the broken relationship, it's important that you let the other person know what the goal of the conversation is.

Let's say your goal is simply to give God the glory through your rela-tionship. Start with that. Let the person know that you want to talk so that God can be glorified by your healed relationship. Remind them of what Jesus said in John 13:34,

34 "A new command I give you: Love one another. As I have loved you, so you must love one another. 35 By this everyone will know that you are my disciples, if you love one another."

Use the conversation as an opportunity to tell the person you love him or her. Now I realize that this is a big step—especially after someone hurts you. But think of God's word. What does it say about love? Let's look at what Paul says in 1 Corinthians 13:1-3,

If I speak in the tongues[a] of men or of angels, but do not have love, I am only a resounding gong or a clanging cymbal. 2 If I have the gift of prophecy and can fathom all mysteries and all knowledge, and if I have a faith that can move mountains, but do not have love, I am nothing. 3 If I give all I possess to the poor and give over my body to hardship that I may boast,[b] but do not have love, I gain nothing.

Thus, since your goal is to glorify God, using the Scriptures as your barometer for pleasing God is a lot more accurate than your emotions. Let's continue exploring 1 Corinthians 13, to learn how God defines love here:

4 Love is patient, love is kind. It does not envy, it does not boast, it is not proud. 5 It does not dishonor others, it is not self-seeking, it is not easily angered, it keeps no record of wrongs. 6 Love does not delight in evil but rejoices with the truth. 7 It always protects, always trusts, always hopes, always perseveres. 8 Love never fails. But where there are prophecies, they will cease; where there are tongues, they will be stilled; where there is knowledge, it will pass away. 9 For we know in part and we prophesy in part, 10 but when completeness comes, what is in part disappears. 11 When I was a child, I talked like a child, I thought like a child,

I reasoned like a child. When I became a man, I put the ways of childhood behind me. 12 For now we see only a reflection as in a mirror; then we shall see face to face. Now I know in part; then I shall know fully, even as I am fully known. 13 And now these three remain: faith, hope and love. But the greatest of these is love.

In the case of overcoming church hurts, I'd like us to stop and focus on verse 5, which says love *does not dishonor others, is not self-seeking, is not easily angered and keeps no record of wrongs.* So that in glorifying God through our relationships, the prescription is given here—to be respectful, to seek mutual rewards and to let go of the offense.

I understand that letting go takes some effort, but you're not relinquishing any power by doing so. Rather, the gain is all yours when you do. Ask yourself the following questions:

1. On a scale of 1-10, how much do you value your peace of mind?

2. On a scale of 1-10, how important is it to wake up each day with a clear heart toward God and others?

3. Do you believe it's wise to hold on to bitterness?

4. Will your relationship with the Lord be better or worse by letting go of this anger?

5. Will your relationship with others be better or worse by letting go of this anger?

Another important question to ask yourself is one that my former pastor often poses to couples dealing with conflict through marital counseling. He'd ask them: *Is it better to be right or to be reconciled?* And although you may technically be right in how you handled the situation before it mushroomed into a church hurt, in how you responded thereafter and in how you refrained from gossiping or bashing the other person, it's important to remember what Paul says in 1 Corinthians 13:3. "If I give all I possess to the poor and give over my body to hardship that I may boast, but do not have love, I gain nothing." So, being reconciled, rather than right, is a way that we can put sacrificial love into practice.

You may be asking, 'Now why in the world would I want to do that—especially toward someone who has hurt me?' Practicing sacrificial love is important because that's exactly how God loves. Remember John 3:16, which reads:

> 16 For God so loved the world that he gave his one and only Son, that whoever believes in him shall not perish but have eternal life.

Think about it. God *gave* His one and only Son. Now, that's sacrificial love. And it's even more pronounced when we acknowledge that we were not in good standing with God when He did so. Yet, as we read in 2 Corinthians 5:17-19, God did not hold our sins against us.

> 17 Therefore, if anyone is in Christ, the new creation has come: The old has gone, the new is here! 18 All this is from God, who reconciled us to himself through Christ and gave us the ministry of reconciliation: 19 that God was reconciling the world to himself in Christ, not counting people's sins against them. And he has committed to us the message of reconciliation.

From this passage we can see that we have been given a ministry of reconciliation. And while this verse is referring to our mandate to lead others to Christ, it also can be applied to repairing broken relationships in the church. We have been given a ministry of reconciliation. That speaks volumes in terms of how we are to walk together as believers because as ministers of reconciliation, we are to continually seek opportunities to lead people into a closer walk with God, rather than driving them away. And if we are truly striving to be citizens of the Kingdom of God, we must model God's character—namely, His sacrificial love, even shown to those who sinned against Him.

The last thing you want to think about

Letting go through sacrificial love also involves a willingness to forgive. And when you're standing in the crosshairs of a church hurt, forgiveness is the last thing you want to think about. Before we step over the threshold from holding on to the offense to letting it go and forgiving, it's likely that we believe that the pain the other person caused us is to be held up as a symbol of how foul and un-Christ-like they are. But think about it, is that really the way you want to live your life?

In John 12:32, Jesus said, *"And I, when I am lifted up from the earth, will draw all people to myself."*

So, uplifting your offense—by sharing it with other people, by having a bad attitude, by ensuring that others are aware of it and by walking in unforgiveness—certainly is *not* uplifting Christ. On the other hand, by lifting Him up, as the One who purchased your forgiveness on Calvary's cross with His own blood, by sharing with others how He rescued you from a life that was separated from God and by consistently offering forgiveness to those who hurt you, now that models His love.

It has been said that forgiveness is not for the other person, it is for you. This saying rings true when you consider how holding on to unforgiveness after a church hurt leaves you standing on the outside of the household of faith, looking in, while the person who hurt you is on the inside, moving forward, as if nothing has happened.

Let's take a look at the process of forgiveness and the steps involved.

a) *Acknowledge that you've been hurt* – This is an important step because denying the hurt now will prolong the healing process. Sometimes we try to be strong and pretend that we're not hurting when we really are. Instead, take a moment to acknowledge that someone has hurt you.

b) *Commit to forgive the person who hurt you* – Making such a commitment means that you're entering into an ongoing process of forgiveness. It may take some time to heal and to have organically positive feelings toward the person who hurt you. But, if you consider your own sins, and how quickly God forgave you, it will make forgiving others easier and faster to embrace.

c) *Stop reliving what happened* – An important aspect of letting go and forgiving is to stop talking about what happened to you, which only serves to bring those old negative feelings to the surface. It's important to remember Paul's admonition in Philippians 3:13-14 about forgetting those things are behind and reaching for those things which are ahead of us—namely, pressing toward the mark for the prize of the high calling of God in Christ Jesus.

d) *Seek ways to avoid a similar outcome in the future* – Do some soul searching. Take some time to explore other ways of handling the situation that caused the church hurt—even if it wasn't your fault. Think about how you would have liked things to turn out in the relationship with the other person if you had the chance to do it all over again.

Without spot or wrinkle

And even though the process of forgiveness is sometimes easier said than done, remember God's instructions to us in Ephesians 5:21, *"Submit to one another out of reverence for Christ."* As this passage continues, the apostle Paul speaks to husbands and wives about being submissive to one another, but compares this submission to the way Christ loves the church. Let's continue reading.

22 Wives, submit yourselves to your own husbands as you do to the Lord. 23 For the husband is the head of the wife as Christ is the head of the church, his body, of which he is

the Savior. 24 Now as the church submits to Christ, so also wives should submit to their husbands in everything. 25 Husbands, love your wives, just as Christ loved the church and gave himself up for her 26 to make her holy, cleansing her by the washing with water through the word, 27 and to present her to himself as a radiant church, without stain or wrinkle or any other blemish, but holy and blameless.

From this passage we can see that Christ is coming back to present the church to Himself without a spot or wrinkle. And, because the Church, the body of believers, is the Bride of Christ, we want to be holy and blameless, ready to be presented to Him without the blemishes or wrinkles of unforgiveness.

A final piece of the puzzle in letting go is to show deference to the person who hurt you. Based on the biblical teaching in Philippians 2:3, *"Let nothing be done through strife or vainglory; but in lowliness of mind let each esteem other better than themselves."*

In overcoming church hurts, you hold the key to the outcome. By taking this Scripture to heart, maintaining lowliness of mind, which is humility, and esteeming the other person better than ourselves, we are set free. Now, I am not suggesting that you take on false humility and allow church folk, or anyone for that matter, to walk all over you. Rather, I invite you to see this verse through the life of Jesus Christ.

He did nothing through strife or vainglory. He came from heaven to die. In Matthew 26, when He was betrayed by Judas Iscariot and arrested in the Garden of Gethsemane, He rebuked the disciple who cut off the ear of the servant of the high priest. Let's read the Scripture together.

47 While he was still speaking, Judas, one of the Twelve, arrived. With him was a large crowd armed with swords and clubs, sent from the chief priests and the elders of the people. 48 Now the betrayer had arranged a signal with them: "The

one I kiss is the man; arrest him." 49 Going at once to Jesus, Judas said, "Greetings, Rabbi!" and kissed him. 50 Jesus replied, "Do what you came for, friend."[d] Then the men stepped forward, seized Jesus and arrested him. 51 With that, one of Jesus' companions reached for his sword, drew it out and struck the servant of the high priest, cutting off his ear. 52 "Put your sword back in its place," Jesus said to him, "for all who draw the sword will die by the sword. 53 Do you think I cannot call on my Father, and he will at once put at my disposal more than twelve legions of angels?

Here we can see that Jesus absolutely was dealing with betrayal. In fact, He was betrayed by one of His own disciples. He didn't fight or allow His disciples to fight. He didn't resist, but instead said, *"...all who draw the sword will die by the sword."* In fact, Jesus admitted that He could have called down twelve legions of angels to wage war if He wanted to, but He was humble. Our Lord knew that His purpose was not to show the onlookers how powerful He was. Rather, His purpose was being fulfilled through submission.

As we read further, we discover that Jesus' disciples ran away from Him, fearing that they would also be arrested. Peter denied knowing Him, as Jesus had predicted, and Joseph of Arimathea—who wasn't one of His close remaining eleven disciples—was the one to claim His body. Where were the others? Jesus had shared the mysteries of the kingdom with them, yet they didn't have His back when He was being beaten and spat upon. How would you have reacted to these so-called friends? Jesus forgave. He not only forgave Peter, ordaining him to teach and to establish the New Testament church, but He forgave all—including you and me—for our sins.

Just as the multifaceted hurt that Christ experienced was part of God's purpose and plan for His life, yours is, too. Thus, I invite you to take this opportunity to follow Christ's example of humility, forgiveness and sacrificial love in overcoming the church hurt that has sidelined you.

CHAPTER 7

CHURCH HURT TRAPS

In the Book of Revelation, chapters 2 and 3, we learn that Jesus Christ assesses the character of churches. Here, He calls seven churches by name and commends them for their good works and cautions them about their weaknesses. Since we know, based upon Hebrews 13:8, that Jesus is the same yesterday, today and forever, we know He is still watching over the church—His Bride—today.

As He confronts each church in this final chapter of the Bible, we discover that Jesus *knows* their deeds. He sees, for instance that the church of Philadelphia has little strength, but has kept His word and has not denied His name[6]. As a reward, Jesus promises to safeguard this church from the hour of trial that is coming to test the whole earth.

According to Revelationcommentary.org, the Lord instructs six of the seven churches that there are both immediate and long-term consequences to their deeds. The threat of immediate discipline for a lack of repentance is given to the churches of Ephesus, Pergamum, Thyatira, and Laodicea. Equally, each church is also warned about the possible rewards and punishments to be experienced at the Lord's coming. [7] Thus, it is imperative that today's churches search these verses, take heed to the consequences and make the necessary adjustments needed to win the favor of the Lord.

---

6 http://www.biblegateway.com/passage/?search=Revelation%203&version=NIV

7 http://www.revelationcommentary.org/02_chapter.html

Sadly, many of today's churches don't acknowledge that some of their characteristics may be displeasing to the Lord. As if offering church and community services were good enough, some churches don't strive toward the excellence in godliness outlined in Revelations 2 and 3. The church at Ephesus, for example, is acknowledged for certain attributes. Let's look at what else Jesus spoke of to this church in Revelation 2:1-7.

> 2 I know your deeds, your hard work and your perseverance. I know that you cannot tolerate wicked people, that you have tested those who claim to be apostles but are not, and have found them false. 3 You have persevered and have endured hardships for my name, and have not grown weary.
>
> 4 Yet I hold this against you: You have forsaken the love you had at first. 5 Consider how far you have fallen! Repent and do the things you did at first. If you do not repent, I will come to you and remove your lampstand from its place. 6 But you have this in your favor: You hate the practices of the Nicolaitans, which I also hate.
>
> 7 Whoever has ears, let them hear what the Spirit says to the churches. To the one who is victorious, I will give the right to eat from the tree of life, which is in the paradise of God.

Thus, a church that is looking to avoid being out of God's favor can look at this church's deeds and follow its example. The Lord pointed out he following characteristics:

- They worked hard.
- They persevered.
- They did not tolerate wicked people.
- They tested those who claimed to be apostles but were not.
- They endured hardships for Jesus' name.
- They did not grow weary.

- They hated the pagan[8] practices of the Nicolaitans, which He also hated.

Here we see that the church at Ephesus had some wonderful things going for it. I'd like for us to focus on the fact that they did not tolerate wicked people.

Doesn't this characteristic seem odd for a church? I mean, why would a church tolerate wicked people? Sadly, many churches not only put up with wicked people, but allow them to hurt others because of their giving. Rather than lose the tithe that these people bring in, the church allows these people—some who even behave as bullies—to continue hurting its members. Thus, finances can be a church trap.

There are myriad church traps, and the commendations Jesus offers to the seven churches in Revelations 2 and 3 provide some guidelines that churches can employ to ensure that they protect both their standing with the Lord and their treatment of members.

When I was a kid, there was a huge push in public schools to stigmatize smoking. That was an excellent program. In fact, I recall one poster that showed a very wrinkled-faced older woman with a cigarette hanging out of her mouth. The caption read something like, "Yeah, smoking really does make you look older." It was powerful since most kids smoked for the very purpose of looking older. Nonetheless, the stigmatizing of cigarette smoking caught on and the number of smokers has been on steady decline. In fact, according to a June 2013 article in *The New York Times*, based upon a report released by the National Center for Health Statistics, from 2009 to 2012, the rate of adult cigarette smokers dropped to 18 percent from 20.6 percent, the biggest drop over multiple years since 2005.[9]

---

8 http://www.lightsource.com/ministry/refuel-with-rick/articles/who-were-the-nicolaitans-and-what-was-their-doctrine-and-deeds--14510.html

9 http://well.blogs.nytimes.com/2013/06/25/why-smoking-rates-are-at-new-lows/?_php=true&_type=blogs&_r=0

This is great news for our nation's health. It shows that the program to stigmatize smoking, started by an initial report by Luther L. Terry, MD, the U.S. Surgeon General in 1964,[10] is making an impact.

Stigmatizing the tolerance of wicked people, those who hurt others in churches, can have a similar impact. It may take time, the way that the decline of cigarette smoking has, but if the church wants to be favored by the Lord, Jesus Christ, it must begin a concerted campaign to stamp out church hurts.

As previously noted, the Bible references the church as The Bride of Christ. And, from the rebukes He handed down to six of the seven churches in Revelation 2 and 3, we see that some churches have a propensity to act outside of the Lord's instruction. I call these churches, Bridezillas, after the reality television program.

On the show, the brides-to-be often are obnoxious, demanding, spoiled and hyper-sensitive. I'm usually pretty surprised that the grooms of these women actually show up for their weddings. And while no church wants to be compared to a Bridezilla, it behooves us all to examine our churches and ask ourselves, 'What would Jesus say about the hurts allowed to go on here?'

When I was praying about leaving the last church where I held membership, I remembered thinking about the Bride of Christ and wondering why she wasn't as pure and holy as I had always imagined her to be. Whereas I had once thought of the Bride of Christ as a beautiful symbol of the Church finally being united to the Bridegroom as described in Revelation 19, she had become to me an atrocity, a living nightmare, a Jezebel.

Let's read the description of the Lamb's wedding in Revelation 19:7-9.

Let us rejoice and be glad and give him glory!

---

10 http://www.cdc.gov/tobacco/Data_statistics/sgr/history/index.htm

For the wedding of the Lamb has come, and his bride has
made herself ready.
8 Fine linen, bright and clean, was given her to wear."

9 Then the angel said to me, "Write this: Blessed are those
who are invited to the wedding supper of the Lamb!" And
he added, "These are the true words of God."

During that time of pain and anguish, it was difficult for me to even
imagine my church as the Bride of Christ, wearing fine linen—sym-
bolizing the righteous acts of God's holy people. Instead, I saw her
as a Bridezilla who had been in a street brawl and had landed in the
gutter. In my mind's eye, her supposedly pure white gown was now
made filthy by the stains of multiple church hurts. The very garment
that was to cover her nakedness, the one that was to protect her from
the elements of the world, was now ripped and tattered. The heel
of her shoe, the one that kept her delicate feet shod with the prepa-
ration of the gospel of peace, was broken off. Her bridal bouquet,
made up of the rose of Sharon, was morbidly dried up according to
my wounded perspective. And ghoulish mascara lines streaked down
her face from tears of anguish. Her lipstick, which had once adorned
the fruit of thanksgiving coming from her mouth, was smeared. Her
hair was a dirty, matted mess, crowned by a shredded veil that had
been dragged through the mud of gossip, backbiting and spiritual
abuse.

What would Jesus say to this Bride? Would He speak to her the way He
spoke to the six churches He rebuked in Revelations 2 and 3? Would he
tell her to go and correct her deeds? I believe He would. Yet, the bigger
question is would she even listen? Had the Bride of Christ become so
arrogant in her ambition for celebrity that she had fallen backwards
and blindly into so many church traps that she had become jaded and
oblivious to the harm she had caused to so many others?

Because my soul was in so much torment, I went to see a Christian counselor during those days. After all, I had been a member of
my former church for nearly two decades, and the difficult separa-

tion was complicated by a nasty church hurt. When I spoke to the counselor, she admitted that others from my church had been also been coming in regularly for counseling. She even indicated that she had to strategically arrange appointments for members and former members of the church to keep us from bumping into one another in the waiting room. And this was a fairly good church, despite the numerous church hurts. But sadly, some people have not come out of good churches and have endured much worse with their church hurts than I did.

According to an article published by *The Wall Street Journal* on January 16, 2014, Vatican officials told a United Nations panel that Roman Catholic Church leaders need to do more to grapple with cases of sex abuse by clergy, but reiterated that the church has limited jurisdiction in tackling the problem. Here's an excerpt from the article:

> Still, Vatican officials added that the church has little legal basis to punish clergy and other church members for sexual abuse.
>
> "[Priests] are citizens of their own states and fall under the jurisdiction of their own country," said Archbishop Silvano Tomasi at the session that was broadcast live on the Internet. The Catholic Church has been badly shaken in recent years by revelations that local bishops mishandled or covered up incidents of sexual abuse over the decades in countries ranging from the U.S. and Australia to Ireland and Belgium.
>
> The Vatican officials told the U.N. Committee that it was aware of 612 new cases of clerical sexual abuse in 2012, of which 418 involved minors.[11]

---

11 http://online.wsj.com/news/articles/SB10001424052702304603704579
324891654814828?mg=reno64-wsj&url=http%3A%2F%2Fonline.wsj.
com%2Farticle%2FSB10001424052702304603704579324891654814828.
html

While the alleged sexual abuse in the Roman Catholic Church is tragic, the insult that is being added to the countless suspected injuries is that the church says it is *limited* in punishing the perpetrators who are found guilty.

Here we find another church trap, sexual abuse. And the church, in this case, seems to be taking a neutral stance when it comes to criminal acts that have allegedly been visited upon its people—God's people.

If you have been harmed by this kind of abuse, consider that the Lord sees and knows your pain. It is His desire to heal you and to help you use this pain to strengthen the Body of Christ. The enemy would have you discard your faith altogether, but God has a plan for your life, and He can use even the most heinous crimes for good.

Similarly, there may be ministers who have been falsely accused of sexual abuse. They are hurting, too. Again, my prayer is that you, ministers, don't throw away or bury your faith because of the wrongful acts of wicked people. Trust that this happened for a reason that's even bigger than your hurt. Consider that God wants to use you as a champion for righteousness in a broader dimension than that in which you previously served—perhaps to support others who have been wrongfully accused. It may be that you would have never have had the passion and commitment for their cause if you hadn't been visited by this type of hurt yourself.

I respectfully understand that you must give yourself some time to heal—and you certainly deserve it—but pray that this church hurt doesn't give the enemy the ammunition needed to quench the fire that you once had in your belly for sharing the gospel and helping others to know the Lord.

False Humility

During the 1980s, Jim and Tammy Faye Bakker had built a tremendously successful television ministry known as the PTL (Praise the

Lord) Network. Let's take a look at the downfall they took because of false humility. Here is an excerpt from a July 2007 article in the *New York Times*:

The Bakker business suffered a crippling blow in 1987, when it was revealed that Mr. Bakker had in 1980 had a sexual encounter with Jessica Hahn, a young church secretary from Massapequa, N.Y., and had paid her $265,000 to keep quiet. He was stripped of his ministry.

In 1989, Mr. Bakker was convicted of federal charges that he had bilked followers out of $158 million by offering lifetime vacations at Heritage USA while knowing he could not provide them and that he had diverted about $3.7 million to support an opulent lifestyle.

The scandals forced the Bakkers to shut down their PTL program and eventually lose Heritage Village through bankruptcy.

Mr. Bakker's wife vowed to stand by her man. When he was found guilty of fraud and conspiracy, she appeared at a news conference and, in tears, sang, "On Christ the solid rock I stand/All other ground is sinking sand."

Three years later, she divorced Mr. Bakker, who by then was serving a 45-year prison sentence. In 1993, she married Mr. Messner, a wealthy contractor and former business associate of Mr. Bakker. Mr. Bakker, whose sentence had been reduced, was paroled in 1994. In 1996, Mr. Messner was sentenced to 27 months in federal prison for bankruptcy fraud.

In the Bakkers' heyday, they were criticized for their lavish homes and extravagant spending on items like matching Rolls-Royces and an air-conditioned dog house. Her troubles with drug dependency and depression made her a target of tabloid headlines.[12]

---

12 http://www.nytimes.com/2007/07/22/us/22bakker.html

Here, the leaders of the PTL Network fell headlong into the church trap of false humility and many people were hurt by it. False humility is presenting the appearance of holiness and godliness, despite the very real sinfulness brewing under the surface.

According to Romans 3:23, all have sinned and fallen short of the glory of God. This means that no one, not even the most dedicated of preachers, bishops or monsignors, is beyond committing sin. However, someone who perpetrates the image that he or she is beyond sin because of leading a successful ministry is downright deceitful.

Yet false humility has deep tentacles in the church. Not only is it exercised by ministers, but by laypeople as well. False humility is a mask that hides the truth about a person's motives and actions. In the case of Jim and Tammy Bakker, they looked like they loved serving God's people. Tammy was even famous for her tears. Yet, Internal Revenue Service auditors have found that PTL founders Jim and Tammy Bakker bought a $592,000 Florida condominium, $67,000 in women's clothes and an $800 Gucci briefcase with money donated to the ministry.[13]

Obviously, this is an extreme and very famous case of church hurt. Certainly, people were hurt after learning that the money they gave to further the gospel and to support other felt-need ministries under the umbrella of PTL was lavished upon the Bakkers for their personal satisfaction. And all this was going on while they were pretending to serve the donors.

False humility comes in many forms. Sometimes it appears as self-righteousness. And while self-righteousness is not an attractive characteristic, it is a church hurt trap because when someone is accused of hurting others in the church, typically the first defense is self-righteousness.

---

13 http://articles.chicagotribune.com/1987-05-18/news/8702060737_1_ptl-founders-jim-ptl-donations-resignation-two-months

Another way false humility shows up in the church is through the requirement of inordinate reverence of the pastor or leaders from their church members. This is a major church hurt trap because it causes members to vie for the pastor's affection and attention. And the temptation is presented for the pastor to play one member against the other. While it may seem far-fetched to some that these emotional games are played in churches, it happens and the results are hurting people.

One of my former co-workers was promised a director's position if he did certain things behind the backs of other employees. He was used as a pawn, a puppet—suddenly "supervising" people he hadn't been officially hired or trained to supervise. He started reviewing others' work, although he wasn't qualified to do. Friendships were damaged. Trust was broken. Still, he continued sneaking around with a hidden agenda aimed at acquiring his director's title.

After a few months of intense skirmishes and sorely broken relationships with other church workers, he wanted to end his role in the charade. The breaking point came when the church leader who was pulling the puppet strings asked him to lead prayer with the very workers he was betraying. I believe that the conviction of the Lord showed up at that point, and he simply couldn't do it. He refused and within a matter of weeks, the leader he had been tirelessly tap dancing for, fired him. Why? Because he finally took back his personal power and said "No" to his demands, and the church leader didn't like it. He was very high up in the church's hierarchy and fully expected unwavering reverence based upon his title.

This ugly need for inordinate reverence shows up in many churches and in many ways. Sometimes pastors or church leaders demean their eager-to-please members by asking them to tend to personal errands. Other times, the pastor will ask church members to make major purchases on behalf of the church because the church's budget can't handle it. Some may ask, "What's wrong with that?" Well, would you make a major purchase for your employer's establishment because it didn't have the budget to cover it? Most likely, the answer is no—unless you're a partner or somehow otherwise invested in the company. And it's okay to support the church beyond the normal channels if you have the means to do so, but when the carrot being held up for the chase is to have you believe you have more faith than those who don't do these things, or that you love God more than the person who is unwilling to take on these extra responsibilities, now we're talking about manipulation.

While I don't claim to understand the psychology behind why we humans get sucked so easily into church hurt traps, I do believe that acknowledging that they exist is an important first step. I encourage you to beware of church hurt traps. And while I have not provided an exhaustive list here, perform your own due diligence before you're gripped in the clutches of a church hurt trap.

CHAPTER 8

CHURCHIANITY VS. CHRISTIANITY

What is Churchianity?

Have you ever heard the saying, "Good is the enemy of great"? What that means is if you're satisfied with good, you will never strive for great.

It's like getting a grade of 'C' in a subject you don't particularly like. For me, as a kid, that was math—almost any kind of math made my head hurt. And as long as I didn't fail, I was happy. And, to make matters worse, I truly believed a 'C' was the best I could do. After all, it was a whole lot better than a 'D' or 'F.' But my satisfaction—actually downright gratefulness—for this mediocre grade ensured that I didn't reach any further than I absolutely had to. Churchianity—deifying your church, pastor, ministry and more—is like that. It's a spiritual plateau that you can get comfortable arriving at because you see that place as the best you can or want to reach.

Now, I don't mean to imply that people who engage in Churchianity are unwilling to work. On the contrary, these are some of the hardest-working people alive. They are the ones who are involved up to their eyeballs in church work. These are the people who rarely have much of a life outside of their church functions. The real problem is that their busy church calendar often blocks them from having a robust and thriving relationship with God. If you practice Churchianity, the Lord takes a backseat to your church title and ministry-related activities. This is because what's most important to you is the honor, leadership, responsibility and sense of significance you receive from others—and not the glory God would receive if you served the church in a more balanced way.

A few years ago, I went to visit a friend in a nearby state for the weekend. That Friday evening, we headed out to meet with some of her friends. As we were driving through the parking garage of her building, she stopped the car to greet a neighbor who was unloading groceries and other items from her car. My friend offered to help, but her neighbor said no, and we drove off.

"That's Sister Carmen," my friend explained as we pulled out of the garage.

"Okay," I said.

"You see all that stuff she's taking up to her apartment?"

"Yeah," I said, wondering where this was going.

"She's taking all that stuff up to her condo so she can spend the entire weekend cooking, making faux flower arrangements and preparing Sunday School lessons for the church."

"That's great," I said.

"Yeah, I really like Sister Carmen," my friend said. "She's super nice. When I was job-hunting, she'd come up to my place to pray with me about landing a job, and she always invites me to her church. I went a couple of times, but it wasn't for me."

"Oh?" I asked.

"No. I wouldn't mind being her friend, but all she does is go to church. Think about it. It's a Friday night. Sister Carmen is a young, beautiful, vibrant woman. But instead of going out to have fun with the girls or out on a date with a man, she's going to use this weekend—like every other weekend since I've known her—slaving away for the church. I'm sorry, but that's just not for me."

Since my friend knew I had worked for the church for 12 years and had recently separated from my role there, it was as if she was disclosing a dark mystery that I was finally ready, willing and able to grasp. She had endured years of my dogmatic lifestyle of Churchianity.

In previous years, whenever she and her husband visited my family for a weekend, our Sunday mornings were a scathing whirlwind of rushing off to church—with me being very, I'll say, *intense* about the prospect of being late because of the additional weight of more people to herd out the door.

What I gathered from our conversation in the car that evening was that I now had a choice to make. I could either continue pursuing a life of Churchianity, like Sister Carmen, or I could make a life for myself that still involved church, but didn't put church at the center of my life and at odds with my relationships and opportunities to serve God on a large scale.

Back then, I believed that anyone willing to walk into church late could not have been serious about God. I also believed that anything that stood in the way of my getting to church on Sundays was a trick of the enemy. So, if one of the kids woke up on Sunday morning with a fever or tummy ache, that was the enemy's plan of attack to try to keep me from church that day. Thankfully, I had the good sense to stay at home, but Churchianity wreaked havoc on my thoughts about how the enemy had sent this attack to keep us out of church that day. I felt the same way about flat tires and snow storms. Although I didn't know it at the time, I took my Churchianity very seriously.

Practicing Churchianity means the church and your work for the church are high up on your list of priorities. In fact, these things come nearly before everything else in your life. Now, please don't get me wrong—I truly admire those people who tirelessly serve the Body of Christ and who are unwavering in their faithfulness and dedication to ensuring that the church functions properly and effectively. The trouble arises when other areas of your life begin to suffer because you're constantly at church.

You don't factor in social or recreational activities outside of those offered by the church. You don't explore other interests outside of those presented by the church. You don't build meaningful relationships apart from those you've developed at church. You hardly take vacations that the church doesn't put together. When you're involved in Churchianity, your children are limited in their ability to participate in extra-curricular activities because you have to be at the church for this meeting or that event. Your husband or wife can't expect cuddle-time with you on a weekend afternoon because the church needs you. And you use most, if not all, of your job's allotted personal, vacation and sick time to serve at your church.

Again, supporting the church with your time, talent and treasure is a beautiful thing, but God gave you a life to be filled with people, interests and pursuits beyond a single one. Think about it, most often when someone is hyper-focused on only one area of her life, we consider that person as out of balance and in need of a more well-rounded life.

Years ago, I used to attend an event called a "Chat & Chew" where women from my community got together to eat and talk with an aim at getting to know one another better. I met a woman there who was going through a struggle in her marriage at the time. She was frustrated because her husband, whom she had married right out of college, hadn't stopped living the life of a frat guy. By this time, the couple had been married for more than 10 years, but according to this wife, her husband was still traveling with the frat, wearing frat attire after work and on weekends and still hanging with his "frat homeys."

While church life and frat life are two entirely different things, this husband's inability to be balanced was causing problems in the marriage. This wife wanted her husband to spend more time with the family. She wanted to be included in his weekend getaways. It's the same thing with Churchianity. Your family members and friends who are not as committed to church activities as you are may not simply be less spiritual than you are—perhaps it's just that their lives don't revolve around the church.

Certainly, you could pick worse things to put at the center of your lives than church. Countless people are band groupies, sports team groupies, celebrity groupies and the like. But, as believers, we want Jesus Christ to be the central force of our lives. We want to be Christ-centered, not Church-centered.

Churchianity is when your identity, ego and spiritual authority are built and sustained by your church activities. The spirit of Churchianity tells you that you are significant, spiritual and making major Brownie points with the Lord and church leaders because you're always there. In Churchianity, your service to God is through the church and not through your life. Unfortunately, this kind of behavior can eventually lead to burn-out and even worse, a church hurt.

Serving God with Your Life

Recently, the world lost a great man. Mr. Hiroo Onoda, died in January 2014 at the age of 91. He had served as a Japanese Imperial Army officer during World War II, but refused to believe that the war was actually over in 1945, and continued holding down his post in the jungles of the Philippines for another 29 years after the war.

Onoda believed that the news that the war had ended was merely propaganda aimed at causing him to leave his post and sacrifice Japan's victory. It wasn't until a student who was searching for him found him in 1975 and returned with a delegation from Japan, including Mr. Onoda's former commander and his own brother, that he finally accepted the fact that the war was over.

While this story may be hard to believe, it's real and Mr. Onoda was not some nut. He was highly trained as a Japanese solider with a loyalty to the emperor and his nation that was unshakable. Let's read an excerpt from *The New York Times*, which reported his death on January 17, 2014.

Hiroo Onoda was born on March 19, 1922, in Kainan, Wakayama, in central Japan, one of seven children of Tanejiro and Tamae Onoda. At 17 he went to work for a trading company in Wuhan, China, which Japanese forces had occupied in 1938. In 1942 he joined the Japanese Army, was singled out for special training and attended the Nakano School, the army's training center for intelligence officers. He studied guerrilla warfare, philosophy, history, martial arts, propaganda and covert operations.

It was in late December 1944 that he arrived on Lubang, a strategic island 16 miles long and 6 miles wide on the southwestern approach to Manila Bay and the island of Corregidor. His orders were to sabotage harbor installations and an airstrip to disrupt a coming American invasion. But superior officers on the island superseded those orders to focus on preparations for a Japanese evacuation.

When American forces landed on Feb. 28, 1945, and the last Japanese fled or were killed, Maj. Yoshimi Taniguchi gave Lieutenant Onoda his final orders, to stand and fight. "It may take three years, it may take five, but whatever happens we'll come back for you," the major promised.[14]

According to the article, when Mr. Onodo returned to Japan, he was celebrated with a hero's welcome for his loyalty and old world dedication to serving his nation. And I agree with Mr. Onoda's countrymen, with one exception. What if Mr. Onoda had returned home in 1945 when the war was over? Think of the lives that would have been saved, think of the children he could have had. Perhaps he could have honed out a new career for himself. Instead, he was blindly committed to a cause that rendered him dysfunctional.

---

14 http://www.nytimes.com/2014/01/18/world/asia/hiroo-onoda-imperial-japanese-army-officer-dies-at-91.html?_r=0

He missed the music, art, theater, technological and medical advances of the 1950s, 60s and most of the 70s. Thankfully, he was found and made to believe that the war was over in time to live out the last 40 years of his life in the real world—and not in a fictitious war zone that he had supported out of a sense of loyalty that had no military merit.

Mr. Onoda's dysfunctional loyalty is similar to the way some people live out their Churchianity. Just as there was no need for him to remain in service 29 years after the war was over—surviving on mostly coconuts and bananas and living in huts without the benefit of medical care and bereft of the freedoms that he could have enjoyed—practitioners of Churchianity are often hiding out from the world and missing some of the good things it has to offer.

One might say that Mr. Onoda served his country with his life, and that's partially true. Unfortunately, he had given his life to a country that had grown in an entirely different direction without him. So, he really wasn't serving his country, but an ideal. Similarly, when you're practicing Churchianity, you're so entrenched in serving your church with your life that you're not really serving God with it.

As believers, our relationship to Jesus Christ is above all else. But it's easy to confuse serving Christ with serving the church because the church is where we celebrate and grow in our relationship with Him. Often, we throw 100 percent of ourselves into serving the church because we love God and don't know of any other ways to serve Him. Yet, just like Mr. Onoda's dilemma, we may end up hurting others, getting hurt ourselves or missing key areas of our growth and development because we're tethered to an unrealistic ideal.

Civil Rights leader Dr. Martin Luther King, Jr. served the whole world, by looking beyond the four walls of his church and envisioning what the world could be like if he used his Christian faith in a broader dimension.

On Thekingcenter.org website, it states that:

"...drawing inspiration from both his Christian faith and the peaceful teachings of Mahatma Gandhi, Dr. King led a nonviolent movement in the late 1950s and '60s to achieve legal equality for African-Americans in the United States. While others were advocating for freedom by 'any means necessary,' including violence, Dr. Martin Luther King, Jr. used the power of words and acts of nonviolent resistance, such as protests, grassroots organizing, and civil disobedience to achieve seemingly-impossible goals. He went on to lead similar campaigns against poverty and international conflict, always maintaining fidelity to his principles that men and women everywhere, regardless of color or creed, are equal members of the human family.[15]

Dr. King could have served God through the church. He was qualified to do so, having been essentially handed a co-pastorate at his grandfather's and father's church, Ebenezer Baptist Church in Atlanta, Georgia.

And he had the education to support his congregation at the Dexter Baptist Church in Montgomery, Alabama. We learn from nobelprize.org that Dr. King graduated from high school at the age of fifteen; he received the B. A. degree in 1948 from Morehouse College, a distinguished institution of Atlanta from which both his father and grandfather had graduated. After three years of theological study at Crozer Theological Seminary in Pennsylvania, where he was elected president of a predominantly white senior class, he was awarded the B.D. in 1951. With a fellowship won at Crozer, he enrolled in graduate studies at Boston University, completing his residence for the doctorate in 1953 and receiving the degree in 1955.[16]

Yet, Dr. King lived beyond the safety of the church. He was imprisoned, was attacked by dogs, endured death threats and more, all for

15 http://www.thekingcenter.org/about-dr-king
16 http://www.nobelprize.org/nobel_prizes/peace/laureates/1964/king-bio.html

the cause of racial equality. Dr. King served God with his life and thankfully he wasn't the only person to make that kind of sacrifice.

Mother Teresa served the whole world as an example of sacrificial living and an unyielding commitment to uplifting the poor through her work and founding of the Missionaries of Charity organization. She left the comforts of a convent and lived among the poorest of the poor in Calcutta, India—sometimes herself starving and going without shelter—to serve God with her life. By the time she passed away in 1997, Missionaries of Charity numbered nearly 4,000 sisters and were established in 610 foundations and 123 countries.[17]

Dr. Billy Graham could have served his church and been an outstanding pastor and leader. But, thankfully, he used his life to serve God beyond one single church.

According to an October, 2013 article by NewsMax.com, Graham held his first crusade in September 1947, in Grand Rapids, Michigan. He would go on to hold over 400 crusades in 185 countries. But in the United States, he has probably received the most media attention for his role as a spiritual adviser to many presidents. His staff has estimated that Graham led some 3.2 million people to faith in Christ.[18]

Clearly, Dr. Graham served God with his life, rejecting the sub-par "good" he could have done by hiding his tremendous gift of greatness in a single church. Instead, he offered it to the whole world—enabling millions to hear and respond to the gospel of Jesus Christ, thereby developing their own personal relationships with God. And while everyone can't be a Dr. Graham or a Dr. King or a Mother Teresa, we all can follow their examples of courage, sacrifice and service. They and many others have exercised their faith in a way that effected lasting and remarkable change.

---

17 http://www.motherteresa.org/layout.html

18 http://www.newsmax.com/Newsfront/Graham-evangelist-final-
   message/2013/10/05/id/529474

You have the same faith and the same Lord as these achievers. I invite you to access it by adhering to the instruction given by the Lord, Jesus Christ, in Matthew 5:13-16.

> 13 "You are the salt of the earth. But if the salt loses its saltiness, how can it be made salty again? It is no longer good for anything, except to be thrown out and trampled underfoot. 14 "You are the light of the world. A town built on a hill cannot be hidden. 15 Neither do people light a lamp and put it under a bowl. Instead they put it on its stand, and it gives light to everyone in the house. 16 In the same way, let your light shine before others, that they may see your good deeds and glorify your Father in heaven.

Here we learn that God wants us to let our lights shine before others. And while the church offers a good place to do so, I invite you to consider using the gifts that God has given you outside the church, too. It takes courage and requires a willingness to serve as the Father's hands and feet. It may mean being rejected or humiliated.

Take the high road in Christendom by developing and pursuing a world-changing vision. Look for opportunities to serve God with your life. Pray about those issues that burn within you so that you can make a marked difference in the world and by doing so glorify your Father in heaven.

CHAPTER 9

MOVING FORWARD WITH GOD

I didn't grow up in the church. Back in the '70s, when I was a kid, we wore pendants bearing Zodiac signs around our necks and patterned our lives around the daily horoscopes.

Back then, my mother was quite young—having had me as a teenager she was the "Hot Mom" in the neighborhood. She was beautiful, trendy and up on all the new music, hairstyles and fashions of the day. It was the Age of Aquarius, the Disco Era was booming, women were burning their bras on TV, America was in the midst of a sexual revolution and my friends and I wore bell bottoms, platform shoes and lots of polyester and paisley. But going to church, for my family and friends wasn't a priority.

Church was reserved for Easter Sunday—not something we did on a weekly or even monthly basis. In fact, the standing joke in my neighborhood was to label people who were habitual church-goers as "Holy Sanctified." This title became so commonplace to us that eventually we didn't even see it as disparaging towards our committed church-going neighbors. But we children shunned the kids in the neighborhood whose parents kept them in the church all day on Saturdays or Sundays and made them wear dresses, suits and shoes everyday—instead of our daily uniform of sneakers and jeans.

"What's wrong with their parents anyway?" my friends and I would ask rhetorically as the "sanctified" kids and their parents marched past the playground on their way to some church meeting or event. "Why don't they just let their kids be normal? Why don't they want their kids to play with us?" We raised those questions on occasion, but we indifferently obliged by never, ever inviting those girls to come outside to play Double Dutch, Freeze Tag or to go to a movie with us. They were weird, different and lived some kind of secret life that we definitely didn't get and certainly didn't want.

Somehow I believed in God—despite the psychedelic kaleidoscope of my youth. It's fair to say my family was ignorant to the culture of Christendom outside of our official, but distant membership in a Harlem Episcopal church. Our attendance there was sporadic to say the least. I don't recall the length of our longest stay, but during that time, I attended Sunday School, sang in the choir and underwent the process of Confirmation there.

I also attended a variety of churches with friends from my neighborhood. The ones who went to Catholic School were required to go to mass every week, so I tagged along from time to time to keep them company. These friends attended only because they had to, unlike the Holy Sanctified crowd, who seemed compelled to be at church each time the doors opened. Other childhood friends of mine attended the local Baptist church, and I jumped on that bandwagon at times, too.

It's clear that I really didn't have any church allegiance growing up and that I didn't understand much about church—how it operated or the culture of church membership. It wasn't until my late teens that I began to attend church regularly—and then it was mostly to be with a boyfriend. Although he had grown up in church, he seemed to have absolutely no reverence for it. In fact, he'd sneak out of service to commit one sin or another most Sundays without his parents' knowledge.

He only went to church to keep the peace at home. His parents demanded it. And I only went because I was in love with him and wanted to spend every waking moment in his presence. One Sunday, though, when the pastor made an altar call—which is the invitation to accept Jesus Christ as your personal Savior—I walked up to the front of the church to acknowledge my pledge. My boyfriend was mostly indifferent about my move. He didn't say anything about it, although his mother shrieked with joy.

Because I didn't know any better, I kept going to the altar every Sunday after that for weeks to accept Jesus. Finally, my boyfriend's mother pulled my coat and clued me in that God had received my prayer for salvation "...the first time."

As you can see, I knew almost nothing about Evangelical church life. And once I did learn how the church operates—by garnering nearly two decades as a member of one church and having spent over 10 years working there—that knowledge became very dear to me. It was as if I had entered a culture that had been foreign to me during the entirety of my developmental years. I finally understood how to "be" in church. Further, I was allowed behind the scenes to see the business side of church operations. I was a marketing and communications person, so I was always in the know regarding upcoming events, long-term church plans, various special projects the pastor was involved in and so much more. After all, the success of many of our programs and events was largely dependent upon promoting them.

Previously, when I was a church visitor, I behaved the way visitors do—taking no ownership for anything and expecting to be hosted and cared for. But going to church is entirely different from being part of a ministry.

Being part of a ministry for me was about serving as an integral part of the church. I took great pride in being someone who made decisions on behalf of the church; someone who had given my natural, spiritual and vocational gifts to the church; and someone who loved ensuring that the church functioned according to the vision of our leaders and founders. At that time, the church meant everything to me.

Once, when I was hosting a friend from college and her new husband at my home for the weekend, my ardent love for the church was exposed in a not-so-positive way. I hated to be late for church—not because I'm a stickler for being on time. I simply hated missing the praise and worship service, which always began at the start of service time. Well, my husband and children were used to the pressure I'd put on them each Sunday morning to get out the door on time, but my friend and her husband weren't quite ready for the real deal.

My first response to their slow-moving, why-do-we-need-to-rush attitude was to politely invite them to just stay at my place until we returned from church. I decided against that because, I arrogantly reasoned, they really would have missed the awesome blessing that my church was. So, I went into overdrive, frantically getting everyone fed breakfast and shoved into our respective cars. Once we reached the highway, I knew they had to follow me, so I kept my foot pressed heavily on the accelerator so they'd have to drive fast in order to keep up. I was serious about not missing praise and worship and my attitude was that they might think I'm crazy now, but they'd thank me later.

Nowadays, when I think about how dogmatic and self-righteous I was back then, I cringe. But I was a staunch church member and employee and cared very deeply about my role and presence in the church.

The Intimacy of Church Life

The church and our relationship to it is a very intimate relationship. And people outside of the church may not fully understand the intimacy many Christians experience when it comes to our church life. Sure, the church is a place where we, as congregants, fellowship together and where meaningful friendships are formed, but it is also much more. It is a place where our spiritual formation is being developed at the same time through our corporate consumption of spiritual principals, giving us an additional bonding factor. The church also is a place where committed members celebrate joys and mourn losses. Further, most church-going Christians bring in every New Year at church and spend most major holidays, namely Christmas, Easter, Mother's Day, Father's Day and the like there, too.

It is typical to see fellow congregants at least once a week, if not more. And our relationships and ties with each other are often very strong—some resulting in lifelong friendships, business relationships and even marriages. But when a church hurt hits you, many of those relationships that you expected to last forever can become frayed, broken or altogether lost. And, because the history of support you once enjoyed through the church has suddenly come to a screeching halt, moving forward son your own can be a daunting undertaking. Sometimes this multi-dimensional kind of hurt, that may include the salt of isolation to your wounds, can be so debilitating that it leaves us "stuck," feeling unable to move forward in God.

Feeling stuck can be a frustrating experience. You may turn your hurt and anger toward God, feeling that He should have warned or protected you from the hurtful people in the church. And when they appear to be thriving in their lives, while you're nursing a church hurt, it's easy to move from distrusting people to distrusting God.

But suppose, for a moment, that God allowed your church hurt because the relationship you have with man is a bit out of balance when compared against your relationship with Him. As believers, God is to be first in our lives. He doesn't want us to lean on the arm of flesh, revering people almost as much as we are supposed to fear Him.

So often we find ourselves doing that because of our relational ties to people. Further, because of someone's title or position in the church or in the kingdom, we quite naturally look up to them—especially if they're well known or acclaimed teachers, pastors, prophets, evangelists or apostles. We tend to have a lot of respect for these people and rightfully so. On the other hand, you may be the person holding one of these titles and expecting people to give you your due respect. And when a communication or an incident doesn't live up to those expectations, a church hurt can occur on the leadership side of the ledger, too.

Consider that your church hurt could potentially lead you to changing your perspective toward people and to being with God in a more balanced way—rather than relating to the church or the people in the church on an equal footing with God. Of course, any Christian worth his or her salt would say, "No, I would never reverence man the way I reverence God." But when you really examine the amount of time you may be spending doing things for the pastor, or at the church or on behalf of the church versus the amount of time you actually spend with God, it may surprise you.

I recently met a man right after he had been physically serving at a church event for almost 36 hours non-stop. Now, you may be thinking, 'Wow, that's a beautiful thing. He sacrificed time with his family. He sacrificed his rest time. He sacrificed time when he could have been out making money.' This is true, but he also sacrificed time with God. And while I can't judge this man, sometimes our service to the church is all about us looking good or looking godly. This means we serve so that we get a little glory for ourselves—even at the expense of spending time with the Lord.

Now, for those who serve, I commend you. Serving your church can be a selfless, often thankless and never-ending job. I will never besmirch the efforts of church volunteers or workers who give of their time, talent and treasure to build up the body of Christ and the kingdom of God, for that matter. What I am getting at is that sometimes God allows us to experience a church hurt because all of our serving and spending time at the church could be about people pleasing or other fleshly pursuits when all He really wants is our full attention on the relationship we are to have with Him. But, the negative emotions resulting from a church hurt, coupled with the loss of your friends and co-ministry workers, your position in the church and your feelings of anger towards God for letting this happen to you could leave you stuck, disillusioned and wondering which way to turn.

Becoming Unstuck

One thing is for certain, God wants you to move forward in Him. Being stuck, stagnant and stiff-necked about your church hurt isn't the way The Lord wants you to handle it. We know from Scripture that God delights in setting the bound free. Being stuck in issues and emotions surrounding your church hurt means you are in bondage. You have every right to feel angry, hurt and betrayed. But yielding these and other negative feelings to God is an important step in getting unstuck.

Again, my former pastor used to ask the rhetorical question to couples who were experiencing difficulties in their marriage: "Would you rather be right or reconciled?" That's an important question to ask yourself in becoming unstuck after a church hurt. The word reconciled here does not mean that you *have to* continue attending, fellowshipping or serving in the place where your church hurt occurs. You can, but you don't have to. Rather, being reconciled means that you have reached a place of peace within yourself and with God about the situation and nothing is holding you back from moving forward in Him.

Once, when I was going through a particularly difficult personal challenge, I was being consoled by a neighbor who had become a trusted friend and almost like a second mother to me. One of the things Mrs. Fowler would often say to, me was, "Cinda, you're marching in time." I had no idea what those words meant. In fact, to me they didn't even line up correctly as a sentence in my minds. Ultimately, I learned that marching in time meant that I was emotionally "stuck" and not moving forward in my life.

Often, the feeling of being stuck is a by-product of dealing with a church hurt. Imagine a car parked atop ice or mud. Although its wheels spin ferociously when you press the accelerator, the car doesn't move. This image offers us an illustration of the way your emotions can render you stuck as a result of a church hurt or any emotional trauma, for that matter. These emotions can range from feelings of betrayal, anger and distrust of people within churches to victimization, grief, depression and more. If left unchecked, your unresolved negative emotions can begin to define your overall perspective of the church. Furthermore, they can adversely affect your relationship with the Lord.

There was a point during my church hurt when I went through an anger stage with God. I was angry because I believed that God was indifferent to my pain. Thinking about that time now reminds me of a quote from Holocaust survivor and Jewish-American professor and political activist, Elie Wiesel. He said, "I have not lost faith in God. I have moments of anger and protest. Sometimes I've been closer to him for that reason."[19]

Because my relationship with God is just that—a relationship—I have to admit that there are times when I, too, express anger and protest about His decisions and what appears to be His inaction at times when I'm facing personal challenges. And similar to the way most children respond to their parents when the answer to their desire is "wait" or "no," most often parents have the best interest of their children at heart; their negative response is usually the right decision, despite the way youngsters may feel about it. This is sometimes how believers behave when they don't understand what God is doing or not doing in our lives. We get upset and question His love, protection and care for us.s

If you are upset because you feel that God didn't move on your behalf or isn't doing much to bring justice to the matter at hand in your church hurt, I encourage you to acknowledge that He truly has your best interest at heart. God is holy and that means there is no blemish in His character that would cause Him to ignore your pain.

I've come up with this acronym for holy: *He Only Loves You*. That means that the only thing God has aimed at you, planned for you and

---

19 https://www.goodreads.com/quotes/412268-i-have-not-lost-faith-in-god-i-have-moments

prepared for you is His love. And that even when it feels as though He's not with you, He is. Even when it seems that He's gone deaf and your prayers are bouncing back down from the ceiling, He loves you. Even when you're standing on biblical chapter and verse and it feels like God is going back on His own word, He still loves you. And even when it seems like He is a respecter of persons—meaning that it looks as if God doesn't love you as much as He loves the next guy or girl—remember that the season you're in, though painful, is His unique way of loving only you.

In order to successfully move forward in God, you must acknowledge that His love is pure and 100 percent directed at giving you the best in life. You may question this statement because of the hard-knocks you've received, including your church hurt. Yet, each time you cry, hurt, wait for what seems like forever for God to bring justice, you are growing both deep and wide. You are growing deeper in your faith and wider in your trust of God and in your ability to stand—the way the Apostle Paul instructed in Ephesians 6:13-14 which reads:

> "Therefore put on the full armor of God, so that when the day of evil comes, you may be able to stand your ground, and after you shave done everything, to stand. [14] Stand firm then..."

Steps to moving forward in God

Moving forward after any personal challenge is difficult. Putting one foot in front of the other and making your life work with emotional pain and bad memories still looming in your mind can seem impossible. Yet, moving forward is an important aspect of your healing.

Step One: Seek God

Consider David at Ziklag. In 1 Samuel 30, David experienced a terrible loss and his men—those who had fought alongside him and fiercely protected him while King Saul sought to kill him—were themselves preparing to stone David. Let's look at David's dilemma:

> David and his men reached Ziklag on the third day. Now the Amalekites had raided the Negev and Ziklag. They had attacked Ziklag and burned it,[2] and had taken captive the women and everyone else in it, both young and old. They killed none of them, but carried them off as they went on their way.
>
> When David and his men reached Ziklag, they found it destroyed by fire and their wives and sons and daughters taken captive. [4] So David and his men wept aloud until they had no strength left to weep. [5] David's two wives had been captured—Ahinoam of Jezreel and Abigail, the widow of Nabal of Carmel. [6] David was greatly distressed because the men were talking of stoning him; each one was bitter in spirit because of his sons and daughters. But David found strength in the Lord his God.
>
> [7] Then David said to Abiathar the priest, the son of Ahimelek, "Bring me the ephod." Abiathar brought it to him, [8] and David inquired of the Lord, "Shall I pursue this raiding party? Will I overtake them?"

Here, we see that David and his men had lost their wives, children, property and the compound where they had been living was burned to the ground. Upon learning of the capture of their families, the men, including David, were utterly distraught, disillusioned and devastated. And if David hadn't been willing to inquire of the Lord, they could have remained that way indefinitely.

That's exactly what I am suggesting you do: seek God. In order to become unstuck from the devastation of a church hurt, it's important that you not only seek God, the way David did, but that you *pursue* God as a key step to moving forward. Pursuing God means you passionately follow after Him. It means you desperately chase God. You long for and run after His presence in your life.

Psalm 42 offers us a beautiful illustration of the poignant pursuit of God. Let's go beyond reading it. Instead, I'm suggesting that you put yourself in the Psalm by envisioning that you are speaking these words to the Lord even as you're dealing with your broken heart.

> As the deer pants for streams of water, so my soul pants for you, my God.[2] My soul thirsts for God, for the living God. When can I go and meet with God? [3] My tears have been my food day and night, while people say to me all day long, "Where is your God?" [4] These things I remember as I pour out my soul: how I used to go to the house of God under the protection of the Mighty One[d] with shouts of joy and praise among the festive throng. [5] Why, my soul, are you downcast? Why so disturbed within me? Put your hope in God, for I will yet praise him, my Savior and my God. [6] My soul is downcast within me; therefore I will remember you from the land of the Jordan, the heights of Hermon— from Mount Mizar. [7] Deep calls to deep in the roar of your waterfalls; all your waves and breakers have swept over me. [8] By day the LORD DIRECTS HIS LOVE, AT NIGHT HIS SONG IS WITH ME— a prayer to the God of my life. [9] I say to God my Rock, "Why have you forgotten me? Why must I go about mourning, oppressed by the enemy?" [10] My bones suffer mortal agony as my foes taunt me, saying to me all day long, "Where is your God?" [11] Why, my soul, are you downcast? Why so disturbed within me? Put your hope in God, for I will yet praise him, my Savior and my God

Let's return to David's plight at Ziklag. We'll begin after God answers David, instructing him to pursue the Amalekites.

[18] David recovered everything the Amalekites had taken, including his two wives. [19] Nothing was missing: young or old, boy or girl,

plunder or anything else they had taken. David brought everything back. [20] He took all the flocks and herds, and his men drove them ahead of the other livestock, saying, "This is David's plunder."

Step Two: Recover what was lost

After taking the first step in moving forward by seeking God, the second step is one of recovery. Experiencing a church hurt often causes you to lose some valuable aspects of your walk with the Lord. In the way that David's wives and children were taken along with other property, a church hurt robs you of your joy, faith, trust and zeal. Recovering these items may seem impossible—especially while you're dealing with emotional pain—but acknowledging to yourself and to God that you've been wounded in these areas is an important part of seeking Him.

David went to battle to recover the things that he had lost. Similarly, I am suggesting that you fight to recover your joy, faith, trust and zeal. You have earned these precious treasures by walking with God. And you need these items to move to your next level with Him.

Do you remember the story about the man who was healed by the Pool of Bethesda? Let's look to John 5:1-8 to revisit this event:

> Some time later, Jesus went up to Jerusalem for one of the Jewish festivals. 2 Now there is in Jerusalem near the Sheep Gate a pool, which in Aramaic is called Bethesda[a] and which is surrounded by five covered colonnades. 3 Here a great number of disabled people used to lie—the blind, the lame, the paralyzed. [4] [b] 5 One who was there had been an invalid for thirty-eight years. 6 When Jesus saw him lying there and learned that he had been in this condition for a long time, he asked him, "Do you want to get well?"
>
> 7 "Sir," the invalid replied, "I have no one to help me into the pool when the water is stirred. While I am trying to get in, someone else goes down ahead of me."

8 Then Jesus said to him, "Get up! Pick up your mat and walk."

9 At once the man was cured; he picked up his mat and walked.

Here we see that, like David, the invalid man was healed and recovered his ability to walk when he took action. Jesus instructed him to take up his bed and walk. God instructed David to pursue the Amalekites. And I would venture to say that God, through the Holy Spirit, is nudging you to reclaim the trophies of your walk with Him.

Step Three: Re-think the rules of connecting with God

In your pursuit of God, it is important that you recognize that the rules of engagement may change now that you are operating as a "free agent," so to speak. What that means is that, in the same way that a professional athlete who is no longer under contract with a particular team is free to sign with any team who wants him or her, you are now free to connect with God under terms not structured by the church.

You may be wondering why this is important. You may be asking yourself, 'Wasn't I always free to connect with God the way I wanted to?' Of course you were, but if your church hurt has caused you to take a sabbatical from regular church attendance or if you're attending but cautious about getting too involved, you may find that navigating the uncharted waters of going it alone is a bit challenging.

I once heard Reverend Dr. Myles Munroe preach a message about what happens when a new government is established. He discussed how the old government, its laws, emblems and customs are usually thrown out and new ones are adopted. Clearly, even in the case of a new political system, some laws can remain the same. But as I understood the sermon, Dr. Munroe was referring to the establishment of new laws pertinent to independence. These are the laws that distinguish the new government from the old government. For instance, in the United States, the First Amendment to the Constitution prevents the establishment of a national church. This was part of a new set of laws that were adopted in 1791 after the country had declared its independence from Great Britain in 1776. . Under British rule, the Church of England was the officially established Christian church and the mother church of the worldwide Anglican Communion.[20] And the First Amendment to the United States Constitution provides that "Congress shall make no law respecting an establishment of religion, or prohibiting the free exercise thereof …"[21] Thus, religious independence was established by this amendment to the United States' newly-adopted laws.

As you pursue God under the new rules of engagement, you may find that some of the rules you formerly embraced are not needed or wanted as you cultivate your relationship with Him. For instance, your church may institute certain times of fasting during the year. As you pursue God under your own prescribed biblical structure, you can set up your own timetable for fasting—even establishing one day of each week to fast, if you like or feel led to do so by the Holy Spirit.

Step four: Let the Holy Spirit lead you

That leads us to another important aspect of the rules of engagement when pursuing God. While I am assuming that your personal rules will include times of Bible study, prayer, worship and giving, it's important to follow the leadership of the Holy Spirit in all that you do. This point is an important one, as God's leadership is impeccable. However, it is also important to ensure that your sense of God's leadership is in alignment with biblical principles and His character.

Often, people who pursue God without a prescribed structure "feel led" by God to do things that may appear odd or questionable to others. There was a time before I was a wife and mother when I felt

---

20 http://en.wikipedia.org/wiki/Church_of_England

21 http://en.wikipedia.org/wiki/Separation_of_church_and_state_in_the_United_States

the prompting of the Holy Spirit to pray for an hour each morning. While on the surface this instruction may not be radical, I followed this prescription that I had heard from the Lord into the time when I was a married woman and my children were school aged.

One day, a wise mother at my children's school said to me, "The will of God is progressive. Perhaps He didn't mean for you to carry that instruction out for this season since you are now a wife and a mother and He's given you new responsibilities." This news freed me. While I didn't view my one-hour prayer time as burdensome, it was certainly challenging to get up each morning at 4:30 a.m. pray for an hour, make breakfast, get myself and the children dressed, drive them to school and not be a bit less than elegant in the process.

Think about Paul's admonition to the church at Corinth when he said, "Every matter must be established by the testimony of two or three witnesses." It shows that having trusted believers in your life who can confirm the leading of the Holy Spirit concerning what you're sensing is invaluable, especially as you work to move forward.

Without Walls

Over the course of 19 years in one ministry, I've dealt with my fair share of church hurts—whether personally or by hearing the ones my friends experienced. Thankfully, most of them were minor, but a few were pretty major. And over the years, there were times when the fight was on and I simply had to work it out. Leaving church was not an option for me back then. But eventually, I did leave. And, like a fish out of water, I really didn't know what to do with myself.

I am a mother who had previously raised her children to be church-goers and suddenly, here I was, not going. Since they were teenagers when I was grappling with the idea of leaving my church, they were generally happy to sleep in. They didn't seem to mind very much that our church attendance was up for debate most Sunday mornings. I slowly began caving in more often than not and we simply stayed home. Then, one day in prayer, I heard the Lord speak these words to my heart: *"You can divorce the church, but you can't divorce Me."*

Those words pierced my heart. I had gone through a marital divorce and it was extremely painful. But I would have never thought in a million years that God viewed my separation from the church in the same way. Yet, He spoke those words to me.

In dealing with your church hurt, you may be considering leaving your church. If so, remember the words that the Lord spoke to me. *"You can divorce the church, but you can't divorce Me."* What that means is that God wants your allegiance to Him whether you're an active member of a church, a frequent or infrequent visitor or someone who's estranged from the church altogether.

Like me, when you gave your life to Christ, you made an eternal decision. Few decisions we make in life carry that kind of weight. But being reconciled to God through a relationship with Jesus Christ is the ultimate decision. It provides an entryway to your salvation and to your eternal life. And while the church may have been the place that supported you in making the choice to follow Christ, the decision you made once upon a time to join your church is *not* an eternal one.

Moving forward with God without being a church member is unheard of in many circles. Yet, it's imperative that you continue walking with God while you sort out your church membership status. Think about it, David worshipped God as he tended to sheep. Jesus spoke to His would-be disciples as they fished. Queen Esther was in the palace of a pagan king, yet she saved her nation through a process of fasting before the Lord. From these few biblical examples, we can see that God can and will speak to you whether you're a church member or not. That is, you can continue to pursue God without the walls of a church surrounding you.

I am not advocating that you choose to leave your church. Rather, I am hoping to relieve you of the fear you may be experiencing about leaving if that's something you're considering. Some pastors and church leaders engage in fear mongering by telling their congregation horror stories about bad things that have happened to people who have chosen to move on and relinquish their membership at that pastor's church. I fully believe that this is manipulation and should be a red flag that your pastor has a controlling spirit.

Leaving your church is a big decision, but if that's the direction you're leaning in, don't go it alone. While I am not a fan of gossip and church bashing, I do believe it's important that you establish a support system during the transition. The reason for this step is that once you enlist others in your search for a new church, they will be happy to begin inviting you to visit their churches. And remember, there will be times after a church hurt when you simply don't want to go anywhere.

Taking a Sabbatical

If you simply need a break between church memberships you may opt to take a sabbatical. That means you take some time off from attending church for a set amount of time. But what do you do during your Sabbatical? I believe that taking a sabbatical means you rest—plain and simple. But resting doesn't mean that you stop pursuing your relationship with God. The same practices you exercised while a member of your church in walking with the Lord should be employed during your sabbatical.

Remember moving into your first place after leaving your parents' home? Prior to living on your own, perhaps Mom or Dad had to remind you to take out the garbage, check that all doors were locked or to turn off extra lights to keep the electric bill down. Once you got out on your own, there is no one to remind you of these things. You either did them on your own or you paid the consequences. A stinky kitchen is a sign that the garbage needs to be taken out and that sky high light bill is a serious reminder to turn off lights when you leave a room. Similarly, this is how you will conduct your life during your sabbatical.

Consider that you're on your own now. The pastor isn't there to suggest that you read the Bible in one year. You have to do that on your own if that's a goal. The intercessory team isn't there to invite you to prayer meetings. You have to do that on your own. You're no longer part of the corporate fast your church is undertaking. You have to institute your own schedule for fasting.

When I left my former church, I joined a women's Bible study at another church. The classes were held during the week, so I didn't have to attend the church services there—which was exactly the way I wanted it. The studies were challenging and meaningful. I was thrilled that I had an opportunity to participate in studying God's word and to pray and fellowship with other believers. I remained in the study for two years and completed my tenure with the women as a group leader.

I am so grateful to have found this Bible Study to support me during my sabbatical. I invite you to find a similar support system during yours. You may not find joining a Bible study as rewarding as I did, but there are other types of groups you can try out. If you're musically inclined, you may want to join a Christian choir or band outside of your former church. Perhaps you love reading. You may enjoy joining a Christian book club. Also, there are some prayer conference calls you can participate in to supplement your prayer life.

Some churches also offer Activity Groups that allow you to fellowship with Christians around a recreational activity. Christian bowling leagues, theater-goers, parenting groups, runners and more are available. Through these groups, new relationships can be formed to support you during your sabbatical. And you can participate at a pace you're comfortable with. If you choose to skip a meeting or two, there's no harm, no fowl. You're a free man or woman with a free will to come and go as you please. This is not to say that you didn't have this right all along during your church membership, but it may be that you didn't have the wherewithal to exercise your rights while you were under the leadership of your former church.

Keys to finding a new church

After your sabbatical, you may consider joining a new church. The best place to begin is with friends and family. The people who know you best will likely want to help you find a church that suits your worship style and tastes. But the key is to let those who help you know that joining a church is your decision not theirs. And even if they believe that their church is the best place in the world to worship, make it clear to them that you will be making that decision for yourself.

After my sabbatical I joined a church after being repeatedly invited by a friend. I didn't think I was quite ready. I had only come to attend their Friends and Family Day service. After service, the pastor—her husband—asked me to join the church. I was a bit surprised since my church background called for a formal membership process involving classes before anyone joined the church. I had only come to one service and had not even prayed about the prospect of joining a new church. The pastor was quite persistent, touting membership privileges and connections within the denomination that could support me and my family in reaching some of our goals.

I refused his advances as politely as I could at first, but he wouldn't let it go. Finally, I said, "Pastor, you don't want me as a member here. I've got issues." The pastor laughed and told me that I was just the kind of member he wanted. He said that people who don't have problems with the church typically don't do anything to make the church a better place. He further explained his own church hurt to me, telling me that it had led him to join the ministry. He wanted to make a change and felt that he could best serve his purpose by becoming a pastor. I was sold. I joined the church that very day. In that one conversation, the pastor had welcomed me, though I was flawed. He had identified with my pain. He had invited me to make a difference. And he had offered me more than a place on the pew.

Your search for a new church may end differently than mine, but I invite you to respond similarly. That is, I want you establish at least a few good reasons for joining your new church. Ensure that the church meets some of your criteria. Perhaps you want to find a teaching church. Stick to that plan. Don't join a church that has a great worship team but no teaching if that's what you really want and need. And let's say you want to find a church that has a multi-cultural congregation and a multi-racial leadership team. Keep that ideal as part of your search. Don't compromise on the things that are most important to you in searching for your new church.

1. Don't check your brain at the door

Finally, when looking for your new church, don't check your brain at the door. Assuming that your new church has all the bells and whistles on your list and you join, it's important that you keep your wits about you so that another church hurt doesn't come creeping in. Sure, people get hurt in the best of churches, but you've been there, done that. You don't have to repeat the lesson again.

If you find that the church is putting too much responsibility on you too early, stop them and let them know that before things get out of hand. If you discover that there is a disconnection between what the church says it stands for and what it actually does, ask for a meeting with someone in leadership to get further clarification.

I joined a church that was extremely diverse, which is one of my must-haves. The congregation was comprised of people, seemingly, from every point on the globe. The only challenge was that the leadership was not diverse. When I asked the pastor about it during a membership class, he was clearly taken aback by my question and was unprepared to answer it. I overlooked the issue because the church met most of the other criteria on my list.

After I joined the church and began serving, the lack of diversity in leadership reared its ugly head. I found out the hard way that this lack had a domino effect which impacted the entire congregation.

Everyone who was anyone in a visible leadership role at the church was of one race. That spoke volumes to the congregants about their perceived value. And because I was a new member, I discovered that my perceived value was affected, too.

Rather than checking my brain at the door, I took an earlier than planned sabbatical. Now, you may be thinking, 'Why didn't you go to the pastor and work things out?' The sad answer is that while it took me about five years to leave my former church, leaving a church now has become easier. The long lasting relationships I built at my former church hadn't been built at this church. I had already survived a church hurt and moved on with God, so I knew that I could do it again. And, I really didn't want to be part of a church that espoused diversity on one level, but not on all levels.

Similarly, in your case, do your due diligence in finding a new church. And don't overlook key factors because they will come back to hurt you in the end. And don't forget to pray about the place where God will have you become a member. He will lead you in the right direction, for sure.

2. Take it slow before launching in

When you do find a church, use care before launching in and beginning to serve. If you're like me, church service is second nature. It's difficult to sit there and be a spectator without doing your part. However, it's important to know that if you jump into serving without setting up appropriate boundaries, you may be heading for another church hurt.

Like the quote from Robert Frost's poem, Mending Wall, says, "Good fences make good neighbors." And this adage goes for church membership, too. When you become "involved" too quickly, there's a chance that you will reopen the healing church hurt wound you've overcome and find yourself right back in a bad situation. Instead, keep a healthy guard up. Remember, the Bible's instruction in Proverbs 4:23, which reads: "Above all else, guard your heart, for everything you do flows from it."

CHAPTER **10**

THE ROLE OF PRAYER

There are some schools of thought that say you should seriously pray about the decision to join a church. Others say you can simply join based upon your enjoyment of one or a few services or because a family member or friend asks you to join. I subscribe to praying before joining, although I haven't always put this into practice and have found myself disappointed in some of the decisions I've made to join churches when I didn't pray about it first.

When you decide to look for a church, pray about what you want, but more importantly, pray about what God wants in your new church relationship. Since Christians often refer to their church relationships as "family," choosing the right place of worship is an important decision.

When my daughter was applying for colleges, she had one particular university in mind as her "dream college." Well, the dream slowly became a nightmare when we learned how much this out-of-state school was going to cost. There was an even higher ranking college, only eight minutes away from our house, that she was also accepted into, but she wanted to be away-away, and not right down the street from Mom. Not wanting to be the one to burst her bubble, I asked her to pray about it and let God decide between the two colleges.

We prayed both separately and together. And God did speak to both our hearts. He chose the college closer to home. My daughter wasn't upset, thankfully. It was a perfectly legitimate way to decide. I knew that God would choose what was best, and He did. After four years of college, my daughter was so delighted with her stay there that she continued on for another year, milking out even more college hilarity. She had formed lasting friendships, enjoyed rich internships, hosted a radio broadcast for two years and spent several semesters as a college TV host—not to mention juggling an eventful love life. And, although the in-state tuition wasn't easy to handle, it was a far sight better than the $40,000.00 a year her dream school would have cost us.

Praying about your church membership is similar. You may have an ideal church in mind, and your criteria list may be robust and chock full of precise specifications, but it's essential that you acknowledge that God really does know what's best for you and that you acquiesce that getting the mind of God on the matter is critical—especially in the area of avoiding church hurts.

How to Pray

When praying about joining a new church, the first step is to seek God. I know that seems pretty obvious, but often we pray about what we want and forget to seek God about what *He* wants. In this case, I want you to ask God what *His* desire is for your church membership.

Step 1: Seek God

This step is something I've always admired about King David, who was a man after God's own heart. That means David wanted to please God and wanted to fulfill God's desires. He wanted to know what God wanted and was bent on meeting those plans. Thus, David often sought the Lord to discern His will, especially concerning a battle he wanted to undertake.

I believe David had seen through his predecessor, Saul, how stepping out on his own understanding could lead to disastrous results. Saul often moved according to what he thought was most advantageous for the moment. And as you know, Saul was rejected by God as king of Israel largely because of his self-serving disobedience.

Saul is a cautionary tale. That is, he is someone from whom we should learn what to *not* do. For instance, let's read what happened when he disobeyed God in 1 Samuel 15:2-10.

2 This is what the Lord Almighty says: 'I will punish the Amalekites for what they did to Israel when they waylaid them as they came up from Egypt. 3 Now go, attack the Amalekites and totally destroy all that belongs to them. Do not spare them; put to death men and women, children and infants, cattle and sheep, camels and donkeys.'"

4 So Saul summoned the men and mustered them at Telaim—two hundred thousand foot soldiers and ten thousand from Judah. 5 Saul went to the city of Amalek and set an ambush in the ravine. 6 Then he said to the Kenites, "Go away, leave the Amalekites so that I do not destroy you along with them; for you showed kindness to all the Israelites when they came up out of Egypt." So the Kenites moved away from the Amalekites.

7 Then Saul attacked the Amalekites all the way from Havilah to Shur, near the eastern border of Egypt. 8 He took Agag king of the Amalekites alive, and all his people he totally destroyed with the sword. 9 But Saul and the army spared Agag and the best of the sheep and cattle, the fat calves and lambs—everything that was good. These they were unwilling to destroy completely, but everything that was despised and weak they totally destroyed.

10 Then the word of the Lord came to Samuel: 11 "I regret that I have made Saul king, because he has turned away from me and has not carried out my instructions." Samuel was angry, and he cried out to the Lord all that night.

Here we see that Saul disappointed God because he didn't listen
to the Lord's instruction. In the words of Frank Sinatra, Saul was a
man who subscribed to doing things "My way." When God specifically said to destroy all that belonged to the Amalekites—including
livestock, men, women, children and infants—Saul spared the best
for himself. He even allowed Agag, the king of the Amalekites, to
remain alive. Saul didn't even acknowledge that God is omniscient—
knowing all things. If He instructed Saul to destroy everything
belonging to the Amalekites, there was a very good reason.

Similarly, when God gives you instructions about joining a church
or not joining one, for that matter, you can rest assured that He has
a very good reason for giving you His direction. And through Saul's
disobedience, we can see what happens when we turn away from
the Lord's guidance and lean on our own ways. The consequences
can be catastrophic. Losing out on the will of God is one thing,
but having God regret anything concerning you is quite another.
As the Scriptures reveal to us, Saul went on to set up a monument
in his own honor and lied to the prophet Samuel saying that he had
carried out the Lord's instructions. Here's what Saul said when he
was confronted by Samuel:

> 20 "But I did obey the Lord," Saul said. "I went on the
> mission the Lord assigned me. I completely destroyed the
> Amalekites and brought back Agag their king. 21 The
> soldiers took sheep and cattle from the plunder, the best of
> what was devoted to God, in order to sacrifice them to the
> Lord your God at Gilgal." 22 But Samuel replied: "Does
> the Lord delight in burnt offerings and sacrifices as much
> as in obeying the Lord? To obey is better than sacrifice,
> and to heed is better than the fat of rams. 23 For rebellion
> is like the sin of divination, and arrogance like the evil of
> idolatry. Because you have rejected the word of the Lord,
> he has rejected you as king." 24 Then Saul said to Samuel,
> "I have sinned. I violated the Lord's command and your
> instructions. I was afraid of the men and so I gave in to

them. 25 Now I beg you, forgive my sin and come back with me, so that I may worship the Lord." 26 But Samuel said to him, "I will not go back with you. You have rejected the word of the Lord, and the Lord has rejected you as king over Israel!"

Here we learn that from God's perspective, obedience is better than sacrifice, rebellion is like the sin of witchcraft and arrogance is like idolatry. Thus, taking heed to the Lord's guidance is significant when praying about joining a church. I'm not suggesting that God will thrust you out of His presence if you don't abide by His will. As you know, we serve a loving God and He forgives all sins. But, why even deal with the consequences of disobedience and the likelihood of enduring yet another church hurt as well? So the second step in how to pray is having a willingness to obey the Lord.

Step 2: Have a willingness to obey the Lord

Let's look at some examples of times when David sought the Lord's direction. Here, in 1 Samuel 23:1-5, David's inquiry of the Lord saved a city:

When David was told, "Look, the Philistines are fighting against Keilah and are looting the threshing floors," 2 he inquired of the Lord, saying, "Shall I go and attack these Philistines?" The Lord answered him, "Go, attack the Philistines and save Keilah." 3 But David's men said to him, "Here in Judah we are afraid. How much more, then, if we go to Keilah against the Philistine forces!" 4 Once again David inquired of the Lord, and the Lord answered him, "Go down to Keilah, for I am going to give the Philistines into your hand." 5 So David and his men went to Keilah, fought the Philistines and carried off their livestock. He inflicted heavy losses on the Philistines and saved the people of Keilah.

On another occasion, David inquired of the Lord after the Amalekites raided the Israelites' stronghold in Ziklag where he and his men lived with their families. The Amalekites had also taken their wives and children as plunder to be enslaved and his own men were prepared to stone David.

In 1 Samuel 30:1-8, David sought the Lord about going after the enemy:

30 Now it happened, when David and his men came to Ziklag, on the third day, that the Amalekites had invaded the South and Ziklag, attacked Ziklag and burned it with fire, 2 and had taken captive the women and those who were there, from small to great; they did not kill anyone, but carried them away and went their way. 3 So David and his men came to the city, and there it was, burned with fire; and their wives, their sons, and their daughters had been taken captive. 4 Then David and the people who were with him lifted up their voices and wept, until they had no more power to weep. 5 And David's two wives, Ahinoam the Jezreelitess, and Abigail the widow of Nabal the Carmelite, had been taken captive. 6 Now David was greatly distressed, for the people spoke of stoning him, because the soul of all the people was grieved, every man for his sons and his daughters. But David strengthened himself in the Lord his God. 7 Then David said to Abiathar the priest, Ahimelech's son, "Please bring the ephod here to me." And Abiathar brought the ephod to David. 8 So David inquired of the Lord, saying, "Shall I pursue this troop? Shall I overtake them?" And He answered him, "Pursue, for you shall surely overtake them and without fail recover all."

The Lord advised David to go after them and surely all was recovered. Similarly, when you embark on a period of praying about joining a church, be willing to act on God's instructions. The answer you receive may be not be what you want to hear in the moment, but the long-term benefits of your obedience will be well worth the short-term disappointment. And the very church you believe is the perfect place for you may be the one where you experience your greatest church hurt if you don't wait on the Lord in prayer.

Step 3: Trust God's direction

Finally, trust God's leading in your decision to join a new church. We all know that God doesn't make mistakes. And following His leadership is the way of peace and prosperity in our lives.

The Perfect Church

Even after you hear God's heart regarding your church membership, it's important to recognize that there is no such thing as a perfect church here on earth. Remember that each human being, whether the sweetest pastor or most humble lay person, falls short of the glory of God from time to time. No human being walks in sinless perfection, although we may strive to do so.

Early on in my walk with the Lord, people used to say, "Even if there was a perfect church, it will become imperfect as soon as I get there." This saying is reliable since no one is perfect. And, because the church is made up of imperfect people, a perfect church cannot exist. So, it's important that when you do find a church that you not become overly critical about its imperfections. I used to visit a church in which the pastor regularly said, "We are not a perfect church, but we will love you with a perfect love." That statement may have been a bit ambitious in the perfect love department, but the sentiment was clear that his intention was to love his members unconditionally, while acknowledging that his church—like every other church—had its flaws.

If your new church doesn't function as efficiently as your previous church, you don't have to point out every flaw. And I suggest you do your best to not keep account of the church's weaknesses. It just may be that the Lord has sent you there to strengthen those areas.

Intercessory Prayer

As I mentioned earlier, one of the churches I belonged to had a wonderful intercessory team. We called ourselves The F.B.I., which stood for The Faithful Body of Intercessors. We prayed on behalf of the church. And one of the things we regularly prayed for was that the Lord would quench the skirmishes that were brewing at the church between members or leaders. While we didn't gossip or discuss any particular issues, we prayed in general that the Lord would intervene and that the enemy wouldn't gain a foothold in the church and cause distractions to kingdom building.

The definition of intercession is "to act or interpose in behalf of someone in difficulty or trouble, as by pleading or petition."[22] In interceding on behalf of your church, you are petitioning the Lord to safeguard the church against any difficulty or trouble that might arise. Avoiding church hurts is something you should absolutely pray about among other things that come against the church, its vision and mission and the people and communities it serves.

As an intercessor, you stand in the gap between what God wants and what the enemy wants. According to Dr. Winfred O. Neely, Professor of Pastoral Studies at Moody Bible Institute, a gap represents a breach in a city's wall made by an enemy to enter the city and destroy its inhabitants.

"The only way to prevent the enemy from entering the city through the breach was for a warrior to risk his life and literally stand in the wall's opening and fight back the enemy," says Dr. Neely. "To 'stand in the gap' means to intercede in prayer on someone's behalf. The metaphor of standing in the gap on someone's behalf in prayer comes from the experience of literally standing in a wall's breach (Ps. 106:23; Ezek 13:5, 22:30). Our intercession for others means that

---

22 http://dictionary.reference.com/browse/intercede?s=t

we are joining them in fighting against spiritual enemies through prayer."[23]

Further, Dr. Neely points to Exodus 32:7-14, where Moses stood in the gap on behalf of the children of Israel after they had crafted a golden calf and worshipped it in the desert on the heels of God delivering them from Pharaoh and his army. Let's see how Moses went about it.

Then the Lord said to Moses, "Go down, because your people, whom you brought up out of Egypt, have become corrupt. 8 They have been quick to turn away from what I commanded them and have made themselves an idol cast in the shape of a calf. They have bowed down to it and sacrificed to it and have said, 'These are your gods, Israel, who brought you up out of Egypt.' 9 "I have seen these people," the Lord said to Moses, "and they are a stiff-necked people. 10 Now leave me alone so that my anger may burn against them and that I may destroy them. Then I will make you into a great nation." 11 But Moses sought the favor of the Lord his God. "Lord," he said, "why should your anger burn against your people, whom you brought out of Egypt with great power and a mighty hand? 12 Why should the Egyptians say, 'It was with evil intent that he brought them out, to kill them in the mountains and to wipe them off the face of the earth'? Turn from your fierce anger; relent and do not bring disaster on your people. 13 Remember your servants Abraham, Isaac and Israel, to whom you swore by your own self: 'I will make your descendants as numerous as the stars in the sky and I will give your descendants all this land I promised them, and it will be their inheritance forever.'"14 Then the Lord relented and did not bring on his people the disaster he had threatened.

---

23 http://www.todayintheword.org/titw_qaindex.aspx?id=84648

Moses stood in the gap between the Lord and the destruction of Israel. He petitioned the Lord to turn away from His anger with the people for their idolatry by pointing to the fact that the Lord's reputation would be tainted if He destroyed the people after bringing them out of Egypt so miraculously through the Red Sea. That's what you will be doing as you intercede on behalf of your new church.

Like Moses, you will be standing in the gap between the enemy's desire to destroy the church and its people and the reputation of God. Similarly, God has delivered the people in your new church from the "Egypt" of the world. Your standing in the gap serves to safeguard the people against the enemy's destruction and to protect the reputation of the Lord.

Praying about your church hurt

Left unchecked, your church hurt can be an opening for the enemy to hinder your success at a new church. That's why it's important to pray about it—so that God can heal that area.

One of the compound names of God is Jehovah Rapha, the Lord our healer. As we know from 3 John 1:2, it is God's desire that we prosper and be in good health. The name Jehovah Rapha is seen in Exodus 15:22-26:

> 22 Then Moses led Israel from the Red Sea and they went into the Desert of Shur. For three days they traveled in the desert without finding water. 23 When they came to Marah, they could not drink its water because it was bitter. (That is why the place is called Marah.) 24 So the people grumbled against Moses, saying, "What are we to drink?" 25 Then Moses cried out to the Lord, and the Lord showed him a piece of wood. He threw it into the water, and the water became fit to drink. There the Lord issued a ruling and instruction for them and put them to the test. 26 He said,

"If you listen carefully to the Lord your God and do what is right in his eyes, if you pay attention to his commands and keep all his decrees, I will not bring on you any of the diseases I brought on the Egyptians, for I am the Lord, who heals you."

Here we see that after Moses cried out to the Lord, He healed the bitter waters the people encountered after they escaped from Egypt. Similarly, God wants to heal the bitterness in your heart caused by the church hurt you experienced.

I recognize that no one wants to admit to harboring bitterness. It's not a very admirable human characteristic and it's often one that we don't easily recognize within ourselves. But without prayer and forgiveness, bitterness can take hold of you and limit your ability to move forward with God and with your new church.

Remember how bitter the prophet Jonah was when God told him to go to Nineveh and preach a word of repentance to them? Jonah was so bitter towards the people of Nineveh, a wicked city that was a rival of Israel and the capital of Assyria, that he boarded a ship headed in another direction to Tarshish instead.

The bitterness that Jonah had in his heart toward Nineveh was so deep that he really didn't want to see the city saved. God had to send a storm to rock the ship so that the sailors questioned who aboard the ship was responsible. When they cast lots and determined it was Jonah, the prophet himself told them to throw him overboard so that the storm would subside. They did so, and the Lord provided a great fish to swallow Jonah, who was kept alive inside the fish's belly for three days and three nights.

Then, Jonah repented and the Lord caused the fish to purge him onto dry land. Let's look at Jonah 3 to see what happens next.

Then the word of the Lord came to Jonah a second time:2 "Go to the great city of Nineveh and proclaim to it the message I give you." 3 Jonah obeyed the word of the Lord and went to Nineveh. Now Nineveh was a very large city; it took three days to go through it. 4 Jonah began by going a day's journey into the city, proclaiming, "Forty more days and Nineveh will be overthrown."5 The Ninevites believed God. A fast was proclaimed, and all of them, from the greatest to the least, put on sackcloth. 6 When Jonah's warning reached the king of Nineveh, he rose from his throne, took off his royal robes, covered himself with sackcloth and sat down in the dust. 7 This is the proclamation he issued in Nineveh: "By the decree of the king and his nobles: Do not let people or animals, herds or flocks, taste anything; do not let them eat or drink. 8 But let people and animals be covered with sackcloth. Let everyone call urgently on God. Let them give up their evil ways and their violence. 9 Who knows? God may yet relent and with compassion turn from his fierce anger so that we will not perish." 10 When God saw what they did and how they turned from their evil ways, he relented and did not bring on them the destruction he had threatened.

This time, Jonah obeys God and delivers the message to the people of Nineveh, who respond by repenting in sackcloth. The king even proclaims a fast and calls for the people of Nineveh to cry out to the Lord.

As we can see, Jonah's bitterness was a hindrance to the deliverance of the entire city. Letting go of your bitterness is an important step to you moving forward with God after a church hurt. Your family members may be the very people God wants to deliver through your obedience. It could be your boss or an unfriendly co-worker or neighbor. See, sometimes it's the people who have offended us that most need our prayers.

Right after I got married, I was working for a boss whom I had followed from a previous company. We had always gotten along well, so

I was impressed that she wanted me to join her at her new company. We hadn't worked closely together prior, so we had a lot to learn about each other while also learning about our new firm.

A third person was introduced to our department of two, and she became the instigator of trouble between my new boss and me. Soon, we were not getting along and I resigned, giving two weeks' notice.

I was bitter, to say the least. Here, I had left a job where I knew the ropes and had joined her, only to be manipulated out of my position by someone who told half-truths to win the boss' allegiance. I had to pray for both of them, but I mostly prayed for my boss. The reason was that my anger was aimed at her. I didn't understand how she didn't see through the smoke and mirrors of my co-worker. And her behavior toward me had so radically changed, that I had to pray to God just so that I wouldn't say anything ungodly to her. I prayed and asked the Lord to bless her, to keep her, to guide her, to direct her and to protect her.

During those final two weeks of my employment there, the managers all went on a retreat in the Catskill Mountains of New York State. They took a hike on the first or second day of the trip and my boss stopped on a jagged hillside, leaned against a tree, and the tree gave way. She fell some 30 feet down the cliff.

When word got back to the office, we were told that she had only sprained her wrist and twisted an ankle. This was a miracle with a drop like that, and off a jagged edge, too. I thoroughly believe that it was the prayers that I had been sending up for her that protected her.

The company asked me to stay on a bit longer while she recovered, and after a few weeks she returned to the office. The Lord had dealt with my heart during that time and when she called to say she was arriving that first day back after her recovery, I went down the street, waited for her taxi to pull up and helped her upstairs—carrying her purse and valise. And I did this every day for those last few weeks of my employment there—even helping her with her lunch and throwing away her garbage. It was quite humbling, but God mended the breach between us during that time and He certainly healed my bitterness.

Perhaps you are harboring some bitterness in your heart because of what someone did to you at your last church. I encourage you to begin praying for that person or persons. Pray that God watch over them and that He lead them to fulfill the plan and purpose He has for their life. You may not be around to hear how God delivers them from a 30-ft. fall the way that I was, but the peace that replaces the bitterness in your heart is far better.

When you pray, remember that God forgave you of your sins. He is not holding them against you. Thus, if you desire to live godly, you will do those things that are God-like, such as forgiving those who don't deserve it and releasing the bitterness you hold against them.

Remember the parable of the unforgiving servant in Matthew 18:21-35? Let's read it together:

> 21 Then Peter came to Jesus and asked, "Lord, how many times shall I forgive my brother or sister who sins against me? Up to seven times?"
>
> 22 Jesus answered, "I tell you, not seven times, but seventy-seven times.[g]
>
> 23 "Therefore, the kingdom of heaven is like a king who wanted to settle accounts with his servants. 24 As he began the settlement, a man who owed him ten thousand bags of gold[h]was brought to him. 25 Since he was not able to pay, the master ordered that he and his wife and his children and all that he had be sold to repay the debt.
>
> 26 "At this the servant fell on his knees before him. 'Be patient with me,' he begged, 'and I will pay back everything.'

27 The servant's master took pity on him, canceled the debt and let him go.

28 "But when that servant went out, he found one of his fellow servants who owed him a hundred silver coins.[i] He grabbed him and began to choke him. 'Pay back what you owe me!' he demanded.

29 "His fellow servant fell to his knees and begged him, 'Be patient with me, and I will pay it back.'

30 "But he refused. Instead, he went off and had the man thrown into prison until he could pay the debt. 31 When the other servants saw what had happened, they were outraged and went and told their master everything that had happened.

32 "Then the master called the servant in. 'You wicked servant,' he said, 'I canceled all that debt of yours because you begged me to. 33 Shouldn't you have had mercy on your fellow servant just as I had on you?' 34 In anger his master handed him over to the jailers to be tortured, until he should pay back all he owed.

35 "This is how my heavenly Father will treat each of you unless you forgive your brother or sister from your heart."

I realize it's difficult for us to see ourselves in the same light as this unmerciful servant, but there are times when we really don't want to forgive the party that hurt us. But, when we think about the forgiveness that God has given to us, and how merciful He has been, is there really any other choice?

As we close, I am reminded of the story of Jabez in 1 Chronicles 4.

Jabez was more honorable than his brothers. His mother had named him Jabez, [c] saying, "I gave birth to him in pain." 10 Jabez cried out to the God of Israel, "Oh, that you would bless me and enlarge my territory! Let your hand be with me, and keep me from harm so that I will be free from pain." And God granted his request.

As a victim of a church hurt, you are more honorable than those who inflicted this hurt upon you—especially if you forgive them and allow God to heal you.

As you move forward in God, I encourage you to pray the prayer of Jabez by asking the Lord:

1. To bless you – with renewed faith and love.

2. To enlarge your territory – that your heart is open to welcoming and embracing others.

3. That His hand will be with you – to lead you as you seek fellowship opportunities with others.

4. That He keep you from harm so that you will be free from pain – that God give you the wisdom to avoid future church hurts.

May God bless you as you move toward overcoming your church hurt.

ABOUT THE AUTHOR

Cinda Adams Gaskin is a writer and communications strategist. She has written copy for books, newspapers, radio, video and television. An accomplished book editor, Cinda has edited some 20 books. She has served as an adjunct professor, teaching public speaking, leadership and promotions writing to college students. Cinda has trained as a Literacy Volunteer of America and as a Children's Church teacher. She holds a master's degree in Strategic Com-munications and Leadership, is certified in Digital Marketing, and provides marketing consultation and coaching services.